KEN WARREN TEACHES

7-CARD STUD

HIGH • HIGH-LOW • RAZZ

D1280501

This book is dedicated to my brother
Daniel Victor Warren
(1956-2004)

Thanks to my friend Steve Vanderkooy of Ocean Springs, Mississippi for his expertise, kindness and patience while teaching me how to use my new $3,000 state-of-the-art laptop computer.

A special thanks to my good friend Ralph Wetterhahn, Long Beach, California for your friendship, advice, example and inspiration.

And, as always, this book could have not been done without my wife Olga's help.

Ken Warren
Kennolga@yahoo.com

KEN WARREN TEACHES

7-CARD STUD

HIGH • HIGH-LOW • RAZZ

KEN WARREN

CARDOZA PUBLISHING

Cardoza Publishing is the foremost gaming and gambling publisher in the world with a library of more than 200 up-to-date and easy-to-read books and strategies. These authoritative works are written by the top experts in their fields and with more than 10,000,000 books in print, represent the best-selling and most popular gaming books anywhere.

Library of Congress Catalog Number: 2007941339
ISBN: 1-58042-221-7

Visit our web site (www.cardozapub.com) or write us for a full list of books, advanced and computer strategies.

CARDOZA PUBLISHING
PO Box 1500 Cooper Station, New York, NY 10276
Phone (800)577-WINS
email: cardozapub@aol.com
www.cardozapub.com

About the Author

Ken Warren has supported himself playing professional poker since he left the Air Force in 1987 and has parlayed that success into a career as a best-selling author of five books on poker: *Winner's Guide to Texas Hold'em Poker, Ken Warren Teaches Texas Hold'em, Ken Warren Teaches 7-Card Stud, Winner's Guide to Omaha Poker* and *The Big Book of Poker*. Warren is the best of the new breed of riverboat poker players, and has the unique distinction of playing in and winning the very first legal poker hand in Mississippi in the 20th century. That landmark hand was kings full of sevens in the big blind position.

Table of Contents

INTRODUCTION

Now that you're ready to improve your skills at seven-card stud, the next time you play, guess what? The winner will be you! You're about to learn how to play and win at seven-card stud and all the popular variations of the game, played in both public poker rooms and in private home games.

You'll learn how to play the classic seven-card stud game and how to navigate your way through the streets so you can then move on to variations like high-low split, razz and home poker games.

You'll also learn how to evaluate your hand as you receive every new card and how to figure out what hands your opponents likely have. Learn the answers to these questions:

- What's the most important single decision you'll ever make in seven-card stud?
- Why wouldn't you want to steal the antes with a very good starting hand?
- Why would you make two pair in your first four cards—and then fold them?
- What's the most well-known strategy tip that you'll hardly ever see in print?
- Why would you call on the end when you're certain you have a losing hand?

You'll also learn how to play razz, which is simply seven-card stud where the lowest hand wins. After reading that chapter, you'll be able to answer these questions:

- What's the most attractive feature of razz?
- What's "The Golden Rule of Fourth Street" strategy?
- What's Ken Warren's best razz tip? (You'll be surprised!)

If you can follow the advice contained in just three basic razz tips you're almost guaranteed to be a winner against the average opponent.

You'd think that once you learn how to play regular seven-card stud for high and how to play razz for low, that you'd know everything you need to know to play seven-card stud high-low split. But you'd be wrong. This is a case where you just can't add the two games together and get a good result. High-low split is an entirely new game and it has its own special strategies and considerations. For example, did you know that high-low split has its own Four Golden Rules that will position you to be a winner if you can follow their guidance?

It's probably true that more often than not, a poker game played at home is more likely to be a variation of seven-card stud, and not stud itself. To that end, I provide you with as many as forty-five different games to learn. You're certain to find several ones that will fit your interest, skill and need for fun.

Knowing how to play stud will come in handy in many social situations. You might be enticed to play in a game at work (or should I say before or after work?), at a friend's house or at a family get-together. And then there's that very important, high priority, regularly scheduled, can't-do-without-it home poker game every Friday night.

Now, read this book and go enjoy your poker game!

You can write to Ken Warren at: kennolga@yahoo.com

QUICK HISTORY OF SEVEN-CARD STUD

The earliest known reference to a stud game played with seven cards was in *Hoyle's Games* in 1867, although it seems most likely that the game was played earlier by soldiers during the Civil War. The use of a fifty-two card deck and the fact that it was so easy to cheat at five-card stud led to the creation of seven-card stud. To make it more difficult to know a player's hand, he was given two downcards to start with and another downcard at the end of the hand.

For the first twenty years that it was played, seven-card stud was known by it's more common, popular name—"five-card stud with two extra cards."

1833 American-style poker had only been around about a dozen years and was in its infancy. The poker deck consisted of only 20 cards (tens, jacks, queens, kings and aces) and only one game was played—Whiskey Poker. It could be played with only two, three or four players because each player was dealt five cards. There was a round of betting followed by the showdown. Highest hand won. There was no drawing or exchanging of cards because there weren't enough cards in the deck to accommodate that. There were two different highest possible hands: four aces or four kings with an ace (four kings with any other card meant that someone else could hold four aces to beat you).

This was the year that American card manufacturers first produced a deck of 52 cards. They increased the size of the deck by adding four each of twos, threes, fours, fives, sixes, sevens, eights, and nines. It was now possible for many more new games to be created and played with the bigger deck than with the older, smaller deck. One of those new games, seven-card stud was, at the time, called by its more popular name—five-card stud-with-two-extra-cards.

1861　Civil War soldiers on both sides taught seven-card stud to the other soldiers in their units.

1891　The first casino poker room to offer seven-card stud opened at the Broadmoor Casino in Colorado City (later Colorado Springs) Colorado.

1920s　Prohibition forced all poker games underground, which in turn caused an explosion in the popularity of home poker games. Seven-card stud was the most popular poker game at this time.

1941-45　Most of the 5,000,000 members of the US Armed Forces probably learned to play the game during WWII which further contributed to its popularity after the war. Poker was so popular that the US War Department (later the Department of Defense) actually hired professional card players to tour the world to teach their soldiers how not to be cheated at cards.

1931-63　Seven-card stud is the only game that most casino poker rooms offer. They introduced Texas hold'em on a trial basis but it took a while for it to gain popularity.

Current　That brings me to today. Chances are, whether you're playing in a casino poker room or in a home game, seven-card stud in its traditional form is waning in popularity while the dozens of variations of the original game are gaining in popularity. However, you need to learn how to play seven-card stud because it is the foundation—the building block—used to help you enjoy hundreds of other poker games.

THE BASICS OF POKER

OBJECT OF THE GAME

If you ask the average poker player what the object of the game is, he would likely tell you something like, "To win money," or "To beat the other players." All of these answers appear to be logical and make sense but you must understand from the very beginning of this book that the average poker player is a lifetime loser at the game and his ideas about the object of the game are wrong.

Would you like to win as many pots as possible and beat the other players in a poker game? Of course you would. And the way to do that is very easy—all you have to do is to play every hand all the way to the end without folding. If you do that, you will:

1. Never fold a hand that will win;
2. Win every time it was possible for you to win;
3. Win the money in those pots and you'll beat the other players.

But you won't be a winner at poker.

The real object of the game of poker is to make the best quality decisions you can with the information available to you at that time. This book will teach you how to do that. Every time it is your turn to act, you will either have to fold, check, call, raise, reraise or check-raise. Your job at the poker table is to collect information, analyze and process that information and then decide a course of action that is best for you.

Once you make a decision and then act on it, you have actually fulfilled the object of the game. This will probably surprise you, but what happens in the hand after you act is not important. It does not matter what your opponents do next and it's immaterial whether or not you win the hand. The most important thing is that you understand why you're making the play and what goal you're trying to accomplish.

BASIC SETUP

NUMBER OF PLAYERS

Seven-card stud has a limit of seven or eight players, depending on how you choose to handle the issue of the seventh card. You'll have to limit the number of players to seven if you want all of the players to receive the full seven private cards (7 x 7 = 49), assuming all players play to the last card. There will be three cards left in the stub of the deck. If you're playing eight-handed, you can deal each player six cards (6 x 8 = 48) and, if all players stay in to the last card, you then deal a single community card in the center.

THE CARDS

Poker is played with a standard deck of fifty-two cards. Some home games also use one or both of the jokers that come with the deck. Playing cards can be made of paper, cardboard, or plastic. The plastic cards are the best because they last longer, they resist marking that could be used for cheating, and you can wash them with soap and water.

There is one additional thing you should be aware of, though, if you're going to add one or both jokers to the deck. And that is, the jokers will usually be clean, shiny and in almost perfect condition while the rest of the deck may be worn and have much less luster. They are often very easy to spot even after being thoroughly shuffled into the deck.

POKER CHIPS

Poker chips are used instead of cash in a poker game. Some of the advantages of chips over cash are that they are easier to handle and count, they speed up the game, they make it easier to split pots, and they make it easier to know how much money a player has in front of him at any time.

The one main disadvantage of playing with poker chips in a home game is that it is very easy for a dishonest player to bring the same chips with him to the game. He can then slip them into the game or his stack, thereby increasing his buy-in without paying for it.

If hosting home poker games is a big part of your life, then I think it is definitely worth your time, money and effort to order custom-made poker chips for yourself. They're really not that expensive when compared to the money you could be spending on other hobbies and they provide a perfect insurance policy against bogus chips. In just one evening poker game, you could be cheated out of more than the cost of a good set of personalized poker chips.

TYPES OF POKER GAMES

Poker is typically played as high poker, where the strongest high hand wins. There are also variations where the low hand wins, and some, where players compete for both ends of the spectrum—the best high hand and the best low hand. All these variations are considered valid and standard forms of poker.

HIGH POKER

In high poker, the best hand, and therefore the winning hand, is the one that is highest on the traditional scale of poker hands. That scale, from weakest to strongest, starts with no-pair, then goes up through one pair, two pairs, three of a kind, straight, flush, full-house, four of a kind, straight flush and royal flush. Most games are played as high poker.

LOW POKER

Poker that is played where the traditional ranking of poker hands is turned upside down and the lowest poker hand wins. Straight and flushes are considered to be irrelevant and it does not count against a player if he has a straight or a flush. In fact, the best possible low hand is a 5-high straight (5-4-3-2-A) which is also called a **wheel** or a **bicycle**. This is a less popular form of poker but still enjoyed by many players. Seven-card stud played for low is called razz and I have written an entire separate section on low poker for you in this book.

HIGH-LOW POKER

This is a form of poker where players look to have either the best high hand, the best low hand, or the best of both. With two different ways to win, these games tend to be wilder with a lot of betting. Typically, the best high hand wins half the pot, splitting that amount with the best low hand. If the player has the best high and low, he wins the entire pot. Or, in certain variations, if a player *declares* that he is going for both, he must win both or he loses the entire amount, even if he has a strong hand on the high or low side.

WILD CARD POKER

This is a type of poker game that allows a specific card, or cards, to take on the value of any other card in the deck. This means that the highest possible poker hand is now five of a kind when wild cards are in play. There are two types of wild card games. The first is where the wild card may actually be any other card in the deck and the second is where the wild card may be used only as any card needed to be an ace or to complete a straight, a flush or a low draw.

VARIATIONS OF POKER

I'm including an entire chapter on the many variations of seven-card stud, almost all of them played exclusively in home games. I have researched what I believe to be the most popular home stud games and have included them in a later chapter in this book. As I said in the Introduction, I believe that one of the most important reasons you need to learn to play seven-card stud is because you need that foundation to learn how to play the countless other variations of the game. Also, you'll be one of the best all-around poker players the next time you play in a home game. This will be especially true if it's dark outside, the big hand and the little hand indicate it's midnight, and there's alcohol involved.

RANKING OF POKER HANDS

Poker hands are ranked the way they are because of one cold, hard fact: The more difficult it is, statistically speaking, to be dealt a particular poker hand in five cards, the higher it ranks on the scale of poker hands. Thus, the strongest hand, the royal flush, is listed first and the weakest, high card hands, are listed last.

So you will see that a flush is stronger than a straight, which is stronger than a three of a kind hand.

Royal Flush and Straight Flush

There are 2,598,960 different ways to be dealt any five cards from a deck of fifty-two cards. Only four of these hands are a royal flush:

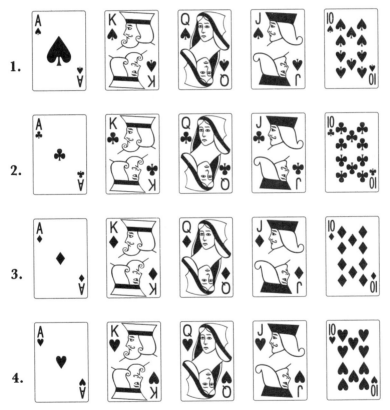

A straight flush is any five cards in sequence of the same suit. A royal flush is also a straight but since it is the highest possible straight flush it is called a royal flush because it contains the court cards with an ace. There are nine other straight flushes and they are the 5-high through the king-high straight flushes.

FOUR OF A KIND

Four of a kind is four cards all of the same rank, such as

or

At first, you might think that since there are thirteen ranks of cards there must be only thirteen different four of a kinds. There are actually 624 of them! That's because a poker hand consists of *five*, and not four, cards. Each of the thirteen four of a kinds can combine with each of the remaining forty-eight cards in the deck to make that complete poker hand (13 x 48 = 624).

FULL HOUSE

A full house is a five-card hand consisting of a three of a kind and one pair, such as a 9♣ 9♥ 9♦ 3♥ 3♠ or

The value of a full house is determined by the three of a kind segment. If two players hold a full house, then the player with the higher three of a kind segments beats the lower one. You are said to be "full of" whatever your three of a kind is. The full houses shown here are "nines full of threes" and "aces full of jacks."

FLUSH

A flush is any five cards of the same suit that are not a straight flush. For example,

is a flush.

When there are two or more flushes in a hand, the flush with the highest card is the winner. If they are the same, then the second-highest card determines the winner and so on down to the fifth card.

STRAIGHT

A straight is any five cards in sequence that are not all of the same suit. The highest straight is an ace-high straight, which is A-K-Q-J-10 of mixed suits, such as

It is also called a **Broadway**. A king-high straight is called an **off-Broadway**. The lowest possible straight is a 5-high straight: 5-4-3-2-A of mixed suits and is also called a **wheel** or **bicycle**. Straights may not wrap around the ace, for example, Q-K-A-2-3 is not a straight, but merely an ace-high hand.

THREE OF A KIND

This hand consists of three cards of the same rank with two other cards of different ranks, such as:

and

are two examples.

Three of a kind is also called **trips**.

TWO PAIR

Two pair is two cards of the same rank and two other cards of the same rank, along with another card that does not match the two pair. When announcing two pair, the higher hand is mentioned as being *over* the lower pair.

is two pair; called "aces over fours," or "aces and fours."

ONE PAIR

One pair is two cards of the same rank with three other cards of different ranks.

is a pair of kings.

HIGH CARD

A high card hand is one that cannot make any of the above hands and is known by the highest card in the hand.

A hand consisting of

would be called "queen high."

These are the standard poker hands universally recognized all over the world. There are other poker hands that are actually called **nonstandard hands** and they're used for, guess what?—nonstandard games, which are usually home games with wild card and jokers. These hands will be covered in a later chapter.

BETTING BASICS

Most games, whether home or in a casino or cardroom setting, require some form of forced betting. It can be an **ante**, a forced contribution into the pot required by all players before any cards are dealt, or a **blind** (as in a **blind bet**) a forced bet required of the first one, two, or sometimes three players in the first round in a game. Blinds are typically associated with hold'em and Omaha and won't be covered here, while in stud games, the first player to act in the first round only is often required to **bring it in**, which means to make a forced bet to get the action going. The bring-in bet must be made by either the highest card showing or the lowest card showing, depending on the house rules. It is customary for the low card to bring it in when playing for high and the high card to make the bring-in bet when playing for low or high-low split.

A bring-in bet must be made regardless of a player's hand and it forces all subsequent players to make some sort of bet or they must fold—there is no checking possible. Antes, on the other hand, are made before the cards are dealt and don't affect any player's options of checking, which he may do if he is first to act and there is no other forced bet required.

ANTES IN HOME GAMES

Imagine you're in a home stud or draw poker game with five other players. Each player has to ante a quarter or a dollar or whatever one chip is worth. Imagine that everyone's having a good time—drinking, talking, walking, not paying attention—you know, like most home games go. There's always somebody who forgets to ante before each hand and it's always a different player. The antes are always one bet short before the start of each deal and nobody can figure out who the short player is. Honestly, this really does describe how most informal home games go.

A solution has evolved to solve this problem. It's simple. All you have to do is have the dealer ante the six chips out of his stack and *voila!*—everybody's ante is accounted for. No one puts up any ante money except the dealer. This works because every player then antes when it is his turn to deal and since the deal rotates and everyone deals the same number of times in the long run, it averages out. It eliminates all the confusion over who didn't ante and it greatly speeds up the game. It's similar to the blinds rotating in flop games like hold'em.

The above accurately describes the most preferred way of anteing in home games today.

I would be remiss to not recommend it to new players and if I don't mention it in the book, I'll get emails that start out with, "Hey, don't you know about…"

ANTES IN CASINO GAMES

In casino games where there is an ante, every player is required to make his own ante bet. This will be supervised by the dealer who will not deal the cards until every player has contributed the proper amount.

BETTING OPTIONS

In a way, poker can be very easy to play because when it is your turn to act there are only five options available to you. You can either:

1. Check
2. Fold
3. Bet
4. Call
5. Raise

That's it. That's all you can do. World champion poker players who have been playing for decades can't do any more than you can when it is their turn to play. Now, of course, poker can be very difficult because knowing which one of these options to choose and why is the hard part that requires some skill and takes some time to learn.

Let's go over what these options mean.

Checking

If it is your turn and no bet has been made yet, then you may "check." **Checking** means to make no bet and pass play on to the next player while remaining active in the hand. In seven-card stud, however, you don't have this option on the first card because the rules of the game require one player to make a bring-in bet, and the opponents to at least match this bet or withdraw from play. The game has to start off with a bet. You may, however, check on the next and subsequent betting rounds.

Folding

Folding is the act of surrendering your hand instead of putting money in the pot. If another player has made a bet and you do not wish to match that bet, you may fold your hand in lieu of playing this hand any further. If you fold, you are out of the game until the next hand is dealt. You may not fold in seven-card stud if it's on you to make the bring-in bet. However, you can fold any time it's your turn to act after that.

Betting

A **bet** is a wager. It is an amount of money that you may put into the pot when it is your turn to act on your hand. When you make a bet, your opponents either have to at least match it or fold their hand. If no one chooses to match your bet, then you win the pot.

Calling

Calling is what happens on the other end of betting. Poker is all about putting up your money in an effort to win the pot. If another player has made a bet and you wish to continue to play your hand and contest the pot, then you must match the initial player's bet with an equal amount of money of your own to stay in the hand. This is known as "calling."

Raising

Raising is the act of increasing the amount of the bet you have to call by an amount equal to the size of the original bet. This is for the typical structure of poker. (There are poker structures where your raise can be for a different amount.) If a player bets $3 and you want to raise, you may do so by adding another bet to the call, thereby raising another $3 (betting a total of $6). Any player behind you now either has to call the $6, raise, or fold. If he has already called the original $3 bet or was the one to make it, he is now due just the $3 extra you raised.

WHAT BETTING IS ALL ABOUT

In poker, you compete for the **pot**, the accumulation of monies bet by all the players, which is kept in the middle of the table. Players will make bets for two reasons:

1. They feel their hands have value and they want to induce other players into trying their luck against their cards.

2. They want to force opponents out of the pot so that the field is narrowed or completely eliminated and they can win the pot uncontested.

To easily summarize 1. and 2. above, you must completely eliminate the opposition or have the best poker hand among the players you couldn't (or didn't want to) eliminate at the end of the betting to win the pot.

THE FIVE BETTING OPTIONS LOOKED AT MORE CLOSELY

Sometimes you don't even have all of the betting options available to you because the action of a player before you can eliminate one or more of those options.

For example:

If You Are First to Act
You can only bet or check. You don't need to fold because there is no bet due to you, nor can you raise, as there is no original bet to raise. If you are playing a game where there is a forced bet on the first round of play—such as in seven-card stud or as in many games where the first player to act is required to make a bet—you will have no choice but to make that bet. But if no bet is required, you have the two choices: betting or checking.

If Another Player Checks to You
There is no bet required to play so you can either bet or check, and pass the decision on to the next player. If all players in a round check, either a new round ensues, or if this is the last round for that game, then all players reveal their cards to see who has the best hand and is the winner.

If Another Player Bets
You can only fold, call or raise. You can no longer check. As they say, make a move or get off the pot. Here is where you have a big decision.

Are your cards worth the money? If you don't bet, you must fold. If you do bet in this situation, known as **calling the bet** or simply, **calling**, you also have the option of **raising** and making the game more expensive for the other players contesting the pot. Now they have to decide if this new cost is worth it to *them* to keep playing.

We'll look into strategies for the different games later to give you insights into how to approach all of these options so you'll have a sense of what to do.

If Another Player Raises
You can only fold, call, or raise again if there has not yet been a maximum number of raises for that round. Typically, raises are restricted to three times in any one round, unless the game is head to head (just two players), where an unlimited amount of raising is allowed between the two players.

Learning the Options is Easy
These options and the limitations on the options are the essence of how the game is played. Fortunately, they are not difficult to learn because they will be repeated in every round of every game of poker you will play. You will learn them easily and quickly through the strength of sheer repetition. It doesn't take more than a few minutes and a few practice hands to learn what your options are.

HOW TO PLAY THE BASIC SEVEN-CARD STUD GAME
Of course, when you have dozens or hundreds of different poker games, the exact way to deal each game varies with the specific game in question. All seven-card stud poker games follow a simple pattern of play:

1. The dealer shuffles the cards and the player to his immediate right cuts them.

2. There is an ante bet made by all of the players. In the old days, each player was responsible for placing his own ante into the pot before the deal. That practice has now evolved

so that the dealer makes the total ante bet for each player out of his own stack of chips. This greatly speeds up the game, avoids confusion over who didn't ante, and since the deal rotates through all of the players anyway, the ante expense averages out in the long run so each player pays his fair share.

3. The players receive their initial cards.

4. There is a round of betting where each player may in turn bet, call, fold, raise, reraise or check-raise. In seven-card stud, the low card showing will determine the first player to act (rather than being determined by a player's relative position to the dealer, as in hold'em or Omaha).

5. The players receive another card followed by another round of betting. There are more cards and rounds of betting until the game is over.

6. There may be several rounds where players receive more cards, and thus, additional rounds of betting—again, depending on the game. After the last round of betting is completed, the player with the best hand wins the pot and the game is over.

7. The deal rotates one player to the left of the previous dealer and the next game begins.

HOW A BETTING ROUND ENDS

Once all bets have been called by the various opponents who have not folded, there can be no raises or reraises in a round. For example, if there is an eight-handed game (eight players), and Player 1 bets $5, Player 2 calls the $5 bet, Players 3, 4, 5, 6 and 7 fold, and Player 8 calls the $5 bet, the betting for this round is over. When play comes around to Player 1, he cannot raise his own bet. Since all bets in this round were called, the betting is over for the round.

However, let's say that instead of calling, Player 2 raises the $5 bet with another $5 bet. Player 8 must now pony up $10 to play (calling the original $5 bet and the $5 raise) or he must fold. He may also raise it $5 more, making it $10 more to Player 1 (Player 2's $5 raise and Player 8's $5 raise).

But lets say Player 8 folds. Now there are just two players left competing for the pot: Player 1, the original bettor, and Player 2, who raised that bet. Player 1 has the choice of calling Player 2's raise and completing betting for this round (Player 2 may not raise his own bet) or Player 1 may fold, whereupon Player 2 wins the pot by default since no other opponents remain. Player 1 also has the option to reraise and push those options back to Player 2—calling, raising, or folding.

Once it comes around to a player and all bets have been called, that's it. A further round of cards will be distributed and another round of betting will ensue. When all rounds have been played for the game—each game is different, as we will show later—then there is the showdown.

THE SHOWDOWN AND HOW TO WIN

The showdown happens when the last card is dealt and when the betting, calling, raising and folding for that round is completed. All of the remaining players left in the game who want to claim the pot then reveal their entire poker hands and determine who has the best hand. The player with the best hand wins that pot.

You win in poker either by having the best hand at the **showdown**, after the completion of betting on the last round of play and when players show their cards, or by default, if all other players have folded their hands (on or before the showdown). If all opponents fold, then the last remaining player wins the pot by default, even if he didn't actually have the best hand.

In poker, you have to pay to play. Any combination of betting or raising by one player along with opponents feeling they have inferior cards may cause all players to concede the pot to the bettor (or raiser).

The purpose of this book is to teach you how to figure out what your best option is when it's your turn to act, and why.

BETTING STRUCTURE

Limit poker is by far the most common type of seven-card stud played, not only privately, but in cardrooms and casino cash games (also called **ring games**). In these games, all of the players have agreed in advance that each bet made cannot be larger than the agreed-upon amount. And raises as well can only be as much as the maximum limit for each bet.

Most limit poker games, especially if you play in a public card room, are played with a 1 to 2 betting ratio. This means that the size of the bets before a specified time in a game will be one unit and the size of the bets after this period will be two units.

In seven-card stud, the small bets and big bets (and raises) are divided before and after the fifth card dealt to each player. In a $5/$10 game, you can only bet $5 before the fifth card; you cannot bet $10. After the fifth card, all bets and raises must be in $10 increments; you may not bet or raise $5 anymore. In cardrooms, the bets double on fourth street if there is an open pair showing in anyone's hand. That is a good rule and I recommend you adopt it for your home games. It helps the hands with pairs fend off possible advances made by hands drawing to straights and flushes.

There are many other limits that could be found: $3/$6, $4/$8, $15/$30, $20/$40, $50/$100, and more.

HOME GAMES

Any poker game can be played for any betting limit and with any ratio as long as everyone in the game agrees before the game starts. The betting limits can vary wildly from game to game so you should be sure to take the time to make it clear before you start dealing the next game.

SOME QUICK TERMS

Here are a few quick terms that you will see used throughout the discussion of the games. Though they are in the glossary, I want you to be familiar with these terms now.

SHORT-HANDED PLAY

Whenever a game has two or three players fewer than is normal, it is considered to be **short-handed**. This is important because fewer players change the mathematics and odds for the game being played and that means that the players must make strategy adjustments. Strategies and tactics that are correct and useful in a full game are not as effective in a short-handed game. Short-handed play is a separate skill in itself that takes a great deal of experience to learn.

STRAIGHT DRAW

A straight draw is four cards in a row with one card needed at either end of the sequence to complete the straight. For example, you have a straight draw if you hold 6-7-8-9 because a 5 or a 10 will complete the straight.

GUTSHOT STRAIGHT DRAW.

A gutshot is a straight draw where only one specific rank will complete your straight. If you hold 9-10-Q-K you have a gutshot draw because only a jack will complete the straight. A straight draw while holding J-Q-K-A or A-2-3-4 is also a gutshot draw because only a card of one specific rank will complete your straight.

FLUSH DRAW

A flush contains four cards of the same suit with more cards to come. Getting one more card of your suit will complete the flush draw and give you a flush.

STREETS

Streets is the term used in stud games to identify how many cards each player has. For example, in seven-card stud, the betting begins when everyone has three cards, which is **third street**. When everyone gets a fourth card, that is called **fourth street**, and so on to the seventh and final card, which is called **seventh street**.

SEVEN-CARD STUD

PLAY OF THE GAME

Every player puts an ante into the pot, and is then dealt two cards face down and one card face up to start the game. There is a round of betting. The person with either the highest or the lowest card showing (depending on the game) is forced to start the betting. After the forced bring-in bet, players may fold, call or raise. In seven-card stud, the low card showing traditionally brings it in.

A fourth card is dealt face up to each remaining player. Everyone now has two upcards. There is another round of betting. A fifth card is dealt face up to each remaining player. Everyone now has three upcards. There is another round of betting. Traditionally, and in most games, the maximum bet allowed doubles on this round. A sixth card is dealt face up to each remaining player. There is another round of betting. A seventh, and final, card is dealt face down to each remaining player. There is a final round of betting.

After the betting is completed, there is a showdown among all active players who wish to claim the pot. The highest standard poker hand wins.

HOW THE ANTE AFFECTS STRATEGY

Seven-card stud is a game where the structure of the game has more of an impact on playing style than most other poker games. That's because the size of the ante in relation to the size of the bets dictates what your style of play should be.

When the ante is very small compared to the bet size, you can afford to be selective about which hands you want to get involved with and play starting hands. You can wait for premium starting hands because the size of the ante is so small that you can recoup those antes just by winning one decent-sized pot.

On the other hand, if the ante is big in relation to the size of the bet, you will find yourself losing your buy-in if you play too tight because the big antes you put into the pot will drain your bankroll. When the ante is big you have to play with looser starting hand requirements and you have to play a little more liberally than the tight player. Tight players prefer to have a small ante so the forced bets don't drain their bankroll.

Another factor that affects your playing style is whether the high card showing or the low card showing has to bring in the first bet. Some games require the low card to bring it in because this helps get an additional player in the game, increasing the action and the pot size. When playing stud for high, the low card brings it in, and when playing for low the high card brings it in.

Good players prefer to have the high card showing bring in the first bet because it's more likely to help make a high poker hand when they hold that card and it might be a hand with which they would have called with anyway. In other words, a tight player who is forced by the rules to make the first bet is a lot happier if his upcard is the K♣ than the 2♦.

STARTING HANDS

The greatest bit of starting hand advice is this: The best hand at the beginning (third street) figures to usually be the best at the end of the hand (seventh street). For this reason, wait until you think you have the best hand at the beginning of the hand before you decide to put bets in the middle. This means you should be selective and you have to be aware of what your opponents have.

There are two other principles that go hand-in-hand with the above advice. Keeping in mind that everyone gets four more cards after looking at their first three, the additions to the above advice are:

- It's okay to start with a hand that you know is not the best at the moment, but has a chance to beat the current best hand before the game is over.

- Drawing hands to a straight or a flush are good cards if certain other conditions are also met.

All of this taken together means that if you don't start with the best cards, you can play other hands if you have a good chance to catch up by seventh street.

TYPES OF STARTING HANDS

The hands in this section are the best of the starting hands. These are the types of hands that experience and computer simulations have proven to be the best. They will give you the best chance of winning your hand when it gets played out to seventh street.

You will start with one of these hands only about one-fourth of the time you're dealt your first three cards. That means, if you play correctly, you'll be folding about three-fourths of your starting hands. Granted, that's a somewhat boring way to play poker, but it's the way to make the most money in the long run.

If you keep track of what you do with every hand, this is what your records might look like:

Fold, fold, fold, fold, play.

Fold, fold, fold, fold, play.

Fold, fold, fold, fold, play.

You get the idea. There are five types of playable starting hands.

1. PREMIUM PAIRS
Aces, kings, queens, jacks and tens.

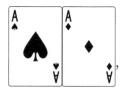  

 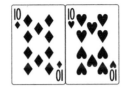

2. DRAWING HANDS

Three cards to a straight, preferably connected (such as 10-J-Q), and three cards to a flush. All three of the straight cards should be 9 or higher and the flush draw should be ace-high.

The Best Straight Draws

The best straight draws are made of three connected cards. They are even better if two or three of them are of the same suit.

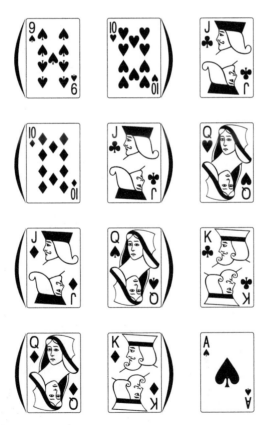

Good Straight Draws

These straight draws have one gap in them, or in the last case, is one way.

The Q♣ K♥ A♦ hand can be either a good or great straight draw. It's very good because you have three of the highest cards and if you miss your straight draw, you can still make the highest two pair or trips. It's a more difficult straight to make because you can only draw to the low side of it.

Bad/Unplayable Straight Draws
These straight draws feature low cards.

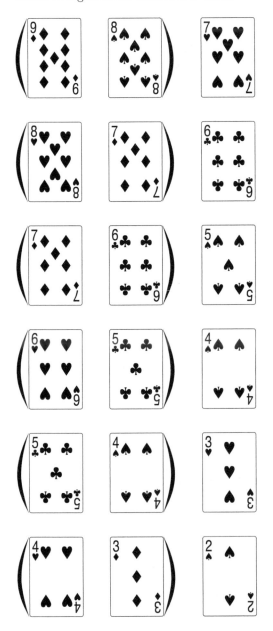

Good Flush Draws

A flush draw cannot be called a good flush draw unless it's ace-high. It's even better if it has straight possibilities.

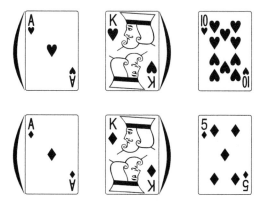

3. SMALL PAIRS WITH A BIG KICKER

The kicker must be bigger than the highest upcard of any of opponents who call the initial bet.

Good Call

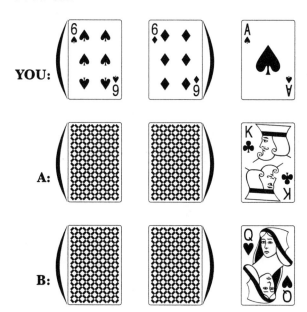

Bad Call

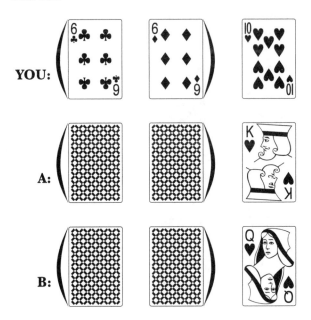

YOU:

A:

B:

4. SPLIT PAIRS

This is a hand like (Q♠ J♥) Q♦.

You have a **split pair** when your **door card** (your first upcard) is the same rank as one of your downcards. In other words, you can see a pair in your hand but your opponents can't.

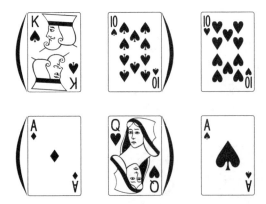

5. CONCEALED PAIRS

This is a hand like (Q♠ Q♦) J♥.

THIRD STREET STRATEGY

Know the Opposition

There's no substitute for being able to predict ahead of time how a certain player will play a particular hand. This saves you time, conserves your mental energy and allows you to devote your attention to other parts of the game. There are players who like to play every time they're dealt an ace, regardless of their other two cards. And once they decide to play, they will always raise or they will always limp in, even when they have a pair of aces. You need to know who these players are, and how they prefer to play their aces.

Understand that seven-card stud is a game of high cards, live cards and big kickers

The cards you play are going to have to be consistently higher than your opponents' cards in the long run. You can't habitually play low cards and be a winner at this game.

Having live cards means that you don't see the cards you need to make your hand in the hands of the other players. If you start with three hearts, you don't want to look around the table and see the A♥ in one player's hand, the J♥ in somebody else's hand and still yet, the 4♥ in another hand. This means three of your hearts are dead.

Bad Flush Draw

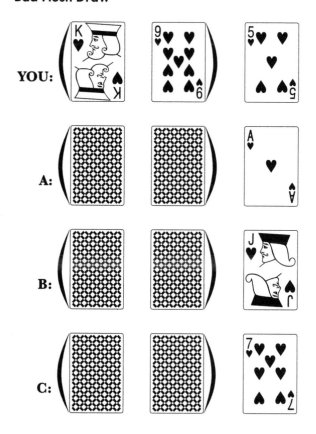

Bad Straight Draw:

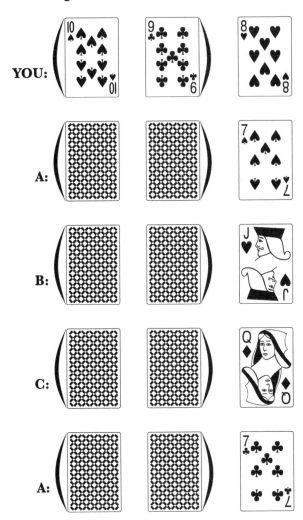

Bad Pair Draw

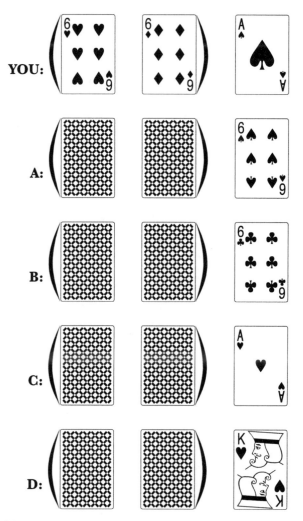

Since two pair is a common winning hand in this game, you need to think ahead and be sure that any two pair you make is going to be big enough to win.

Remember that any small two pair only makes a small full house. If you start with a hand like 4♠ 5♥ 4♦, you are doubly handicapped, even though you might have the highest hand at the moment. You have a low pair, you have a low kicker and if you make two pair, it will only be fives and fours. If you see another 4 or 5 around the board, you are really in trouble. Good players pass hands like this most of the time.

Bad Call

Sometimes you have to bring in the initial bet with this hand, and when no one raises, you make a hand like this on fourth street:

If you look around and see another 4 or 5, you have a bad hand. Your chances of improving are terrible. If you see two or more fours or fives, you have a terrible hand. In view of the fact that you have so little money invested in the hand and the bets double on the next round, you should almost always throw this hand away when faced with a bet.

When you have the best starting hand, you want players out rather than in

If you start with A♣ Q♥ A♦ you will most likely finish with two high pair or trips. With a hand like that you want to play against fewer players rather than many. Don't just call with this hand. Raise! Narrow the field, make it incorrect for straight and flush draws to try to run you down.

Too many players like to limp in with this hand because they think they'll win a bigger pot with more players in the hand. This is wrong!

A lot of players in the hand increases the likelihood that someone will make a straight or a flush against your two pair or trips. You should always raise to give the drawing hands the wrong odds to play against your premium pair. If you raise, the only hands that should be able to call you will be other pairs. This is good for you because you will win these contests most of the time.

It is better to win a small pot than to lose a big one. The biggest benefit of raising with an ace showing is that in the future, you won't always have that pair of aces. Sometimes you'll have two other high cards that are overcards to all the other upcards on board. Sometimes you will have a pair in the pocket and sometimes you will have a three-flush in the suit of your ace.

This means that when you raise with the ace showing, your opponents won't know if you have A♦ J♥ A♣, K♥ Q♦ A♣, 5♠ 5♣ A♥ or 9♣ 3♣ A♣. This adds an element of deception to your play and makes it harder for opponents to read your hands. This in turn causes them to make mistakes when playing against you and leads to profits.

Raise when you have a concealed pair and the highest upcard

If you have 7♥ 7♦ Q♥ you should raise if you don't see any other upcards higher than your queen. This gives you the best chance to win the hand.

Raise when you have (7♠ 7♦) Q ♥ and the other player's upcards are J♠, 9♥ 6♦ and 2♦. Do not raise if their upcards are aces or kings.

When calling a raise, your own side card is very important

You can call a raise with J♠ 8♦ 8♥ if the raiser has an upcard lower than your jack but you should fold if his upcard is higher than your jack.

Call a raise with

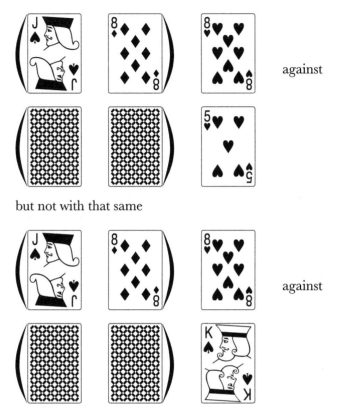

against

but not with that same

against

***When you have a split pair such as (J♠ 6♣) 6♥ you can raise
against one higher upcard but not more than one***

A player showing an ace, king or queen won't necessarily be paired
with that upcard and he will often fold, making your hand high. This is
not a profitable strategy if you're facing more than two upcards. Don't
forget to look around the board. If you have a pair of kings and you
see three aces up on third street, it's a good bet that no player has the
case ace to make a pair, making your kings currently the best hand.
Also, if you have Q♠ Q♣ X and your opponent's upcard is the K♥
you might ordinarily be worried that he has a pair of kings. But—if
you look around the board and you see two other kings face up, then

you know it's unlikely he has the case king. If he calls your bet, it's probably because he has some hand other than kings.

You can raise with

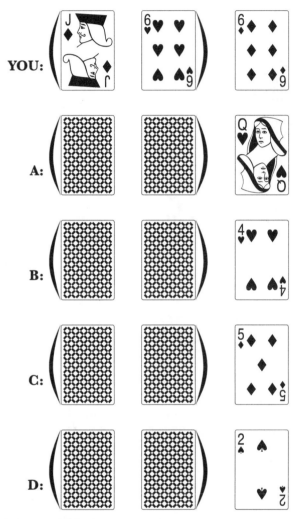

but not with

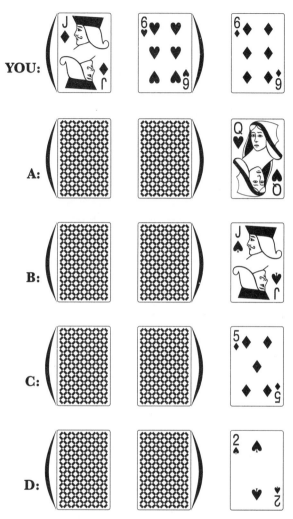

Just the addition of one extra overcard to your door card makes a raise unprofitable. Remember, the more cards there are higher than your 6♦, the more likely it is you'll be called by a higher pair.

A pair of tens is a much better hand to start with than a pair of nines, even though they are close in strength

That's because you need a 5 or a 10 to make a straight. If you have two tens in your hand that greatly reduces the chance that someone will make a straight to beat you.

You will win 30 to 40 percent more hands when you have (A♠ 10♣) 10♦ than when you have (A♠ 9♣) 9♦.

Starting with a pair of tens, jacks, queens, kings or aces

Your usual strategy will be to raise and do whatever it takes to drive players out of the hand. These high pairs play best against fewer rather than many players. You will usually have the best hand at this point and only one or two players will have a hard time beating you by the last card.

When you have one of the following hands, you have the best chance of winning if you can play it against only one or two other players. High pairs do not normally turn into straights and flushes; they are more likely to improve to two pair or trips. High pair hands will do fine against one or two opponents, but not against five opponents.

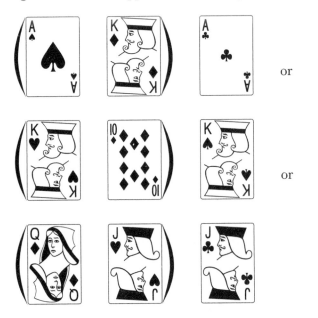

or

or

Starting with three of a kind

You will be dealt trips only once every 425 hands. But understanding how to play them is important. You should usually do whatever looks natural for the upcard you have. If you start with (A♥ A♦) A♣ you should raise because that will not draw any suspicion. If you start with (5♠ 5♣) 5♦ then you should just call. However, not all rules are written in stone. If you think you can get in a raise with a 5♦ showing, then by all means do so. It depends on your opponents and the game conditions.

Rolled up trips will win a large share of hands regardless of how you play them, how many players you play against, whether they're deuces or aces and how many outs you have. There's almost no wrong way to play rolled up trips; however, some strategies are slightly better than others. Your goal from the start of the hand is figure out how to maximize the profit in the hand. Take in all the information you can and then adjust your strategy as the hand progresses.

Be careful, however, not to get so excited that you give away your hand immediately on third street.

When you start with rolled-up trips, you will improve to a full house or quads a whopping 40 percent of the time.

Small pairs are not a strong enough hand to bet on early in the game

Their strength comes from the fact that they have deception value if they are concealed and it is easy for opponents to misread your hand. If you have 4♦ 4♣ K♥ and you get another four, your hand will be very well disguised.

is not normally going to win the hand unless it immediately turns into

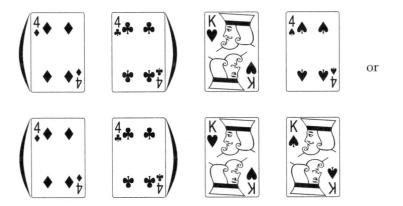

Do not play small straight draws

If you do, it means that you started with three small cards and making the straight will usually be your only way to win the hand. That is not going to happen often enough to justify playing those low cards. Most of the time you will end up with a small pair or twos and that will make you a loser in the long run.

The above hand will not turn into a straight often enough to win, and when it does win the hand, it won't win enough money to make up for the times you played this hand and lost.

Some players like to limp in when they start with the best pair, usually aces or kings

Take the time to remember who these players are because this will help you read their hands later. When you can positively put a player on a specific pair or two pair, you can make a lot of money from him by knowing when to raise and check-raise. You also know when his cards are live or dead and he won't know that you know that.

If you have (A♦ J♦) A♥ and you do not raise to eliminate players, the size of this mistake is directly proportional to the number of players you could have knocked out but didn't.

Three big straight flush cards are a great starting hand, but remember, you will not actually make the straight flush most of the time
You have to pay a little more attention because now you must look not only for flush cards and straight cards, but your high cards as well. Low flush draws usually win only by actually making the flush—not by making a backdoor one or two pair.

will finish the hand by making two pair or trips more than any other hand (such as straights or flushes). For that reason, a low straight flush hand such as

is not nearly as good as it looks since your most likely final hand will be a low two pair or trips. Most good players actually fold this type of hand on third street, especially against a small field.

When a game is short-handed, the value of all pairs goes up while the value of straight and flush draws goes down
That's because you will usually not get the right odds to draw to straights and flushes and when you miss, anyone left in the hand with a pair can pick you off.

is just as good as

in a short-handed game. And

is just as good as

Having slightly fewer players in a game means that slightly weaker hands, on average, will win the pot. You don't need a monster hand to win two- or three-handed.

Not all drawing hands are equal

Whether or not you should draw to a straight or flush depends on your position, the pot odds you're getting and your door card. If you are to the left of the highest card on board, you will usually have to call a bet to draw. If you are heads-up, you won't be getting the correct odds to play. If your door card, your first face-upcard, is dead, the other players will correctly deduce that you might be on a draw.

If you have

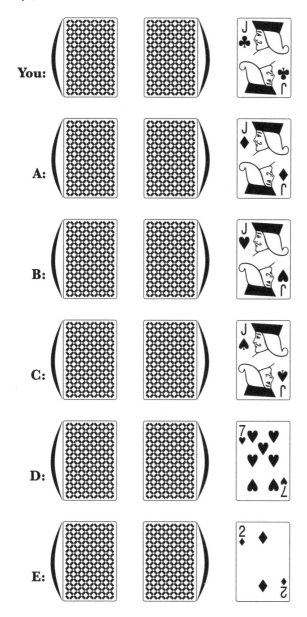

the other players will correctly deduce that you're on a draw. Sure, you could have a concealed pair, but it's about 15-1 against it.

Ante stealing is a big part of the game when the ante is big compared to the size of the initial bet

If this is the case, you should raise a lot more often on third street with any playable hand if you are the first to enter the pot. The bigger the pot, the more correct it is to play looser. That means you can raise with hands you would usually call with and you can call with some hands that you might often fold.

If there's $5 in the pot and the most you can bet is $5, then it's correct for the other players to call you with much weaker, but still reasonable, hands. When the antes are big compared to the size of the bets, you're often just building a pot.

On the other hand, if there's only $2 in the pot, then a $10 bet is likely to succeed in stealing the antes. The relationship between the size of the first bet and the size of the ante-only pot is what determines the probable success of ante-stealing attempts. The bigger the disparity, the bigger the chance of a successful steal.

You should think about stealing the antes with only your decent, but second-best, starting hands. This advice is probably a surprise to you. "Why wouldn't I want to steal the antes with my best hands?" you might ask. It's because your best hands earn more money if you play them to the end against an opponent or two. Remember, that's the object of the game! Your second-best hands make more money if you can bet and win the pot right there.

Steal the antes with hands like

and

But don't try to steal just the antes with hands like

or

However, you can raise with these hands to build a pot you expect to win if you think you'll be called.

FOURTH STREET STRATEGY

After the smoke has cleared on third street and you see who has survived the initial betting round, you might have an idea of what some of the other players have started with. And maybe not. The card that comes on fourth street will give you a clue about everyone's hand because you will get to see how it relates to their first upcard and how they feel about that relationship. This is the beginning of being able to read opponents' hands.

They will be looking at you and your cards, too. This is how you should proceed on fourth street:

You're going to have to compare your new card and new hand to that of your opponent's

Lets look at your hand first. After you get your fourth card, you're going to have one of these types of hands:

1. No Pair (which might include a straight or a flush draw)

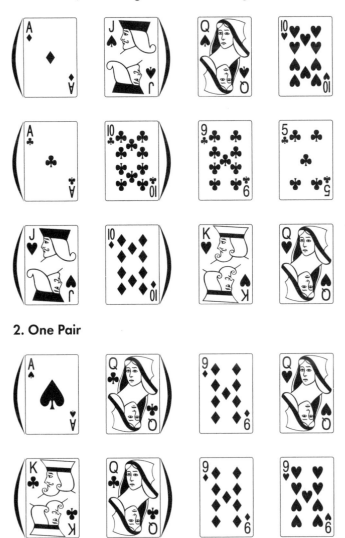

2. One Pair

3. Your Door Card is Paired

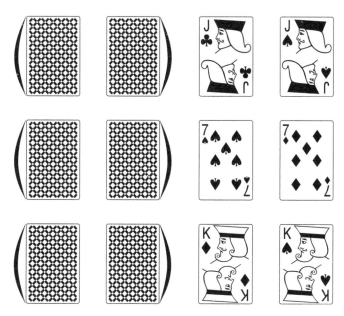

You paired your door card and have an open pair showing. Only you know if this made you trips or not. As far as the other players know, any of the three above hands could be one pair, two pair, trips, or even quads.

4. Two Pair

5. Trips

6. Four of a Kind (also known as quads)

ANALYZING THE SIX TYPES OF HANDS

NO PAIR ON FOURTH STREET

Do not draw to an inside straight no-pair hand unless everyone else has smaller cards than you

As an obvious example, it does not pay to draw to 4♦ 5♠ 7♣ 8♥ when the other player is showing (X X) K♠ Q♥. If you started without a pair and still don't have a pair on fourth street, it will usually be because you were looking for the straight or flush draw. The fourth street card will improve your straight draw about 25 percent of the time and it will improve your flush draw only about 20 percent of the time. That's because there are 12 cards that will improve a straight draw but there are only 10 cards that will improve a flush draw. One of the added benefits of drawing to a flush and missing on fourth street is that you will often pick up a card that will add a straight draw to your flush draw.

is not a good draw when you're looking at

or

Low straight draws just don't perform well against higher straight draws. That's because, from a mathematical standpoint, both draws will often not get there and the higher cards will beat the lower cards, even if they both make a pair.

If you do draw to a gutshot straight, all four of your cards must be live

Three live cards are not enough. The reason is, if you're playing high cards, your opponents will be, too. If you need a big card to make a straight, there's a good chance one of those cards is already in the hands of your opponent, even if you don't see it. If you actually see one of your **out cards**, cards that will actually improve your hand, on board, then it's very likely that there are two of them out—one seen and one unseen by you. That means you really only have two outs and that's not enough.

If you have

(you should usually fold if you can see an ace or a 10 on the board. Since this implies that these players have a pair of aces and tens that means you actually have fewer outs than direct observation tells you.

Beware of players who catch an ace or king on fourth street

Good players just generally (and correctly) prefer high cards. These high cards will be concealed as two of their first downcards. It just makes sense that an ace or a king on fourth street would be of help. Opponents who catch an ace or king on fourth street often will have made a pair of aces or kings. Look at it from the other point of view: Wouldn't you usually like to have an ace or a king on fourth street? If you're playing properly, you would.

A player showing

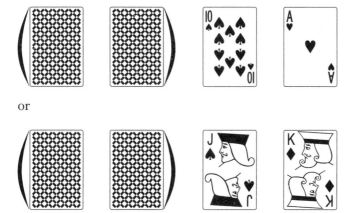

or

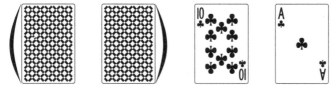

usually made a split pair of aces or kings on fourth street.

Be wary when your opponents catch a suited overcard to their door card on fourth street

It just makes sense that it would probably help them. A suited overcard helps every straight and flush draw and every pair become a higher two pair.

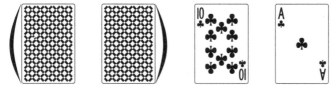

The A♣ just possibly helped make a pair of aces, aces and tens (two pair), a three-card straight or a four-card straight draw. This player also has three more cards to come with which to make a straight or a flush. All you have to do is ask yourself, "How does an ace on fourth street hurt my opponent?" You should realize that most of the time it doesn't hurt.

Watch for players who switch the order of their third- and fourth street cards

This sometimes occurs in home games and you should probably have a rule against it. Players switch cards because they think it helps them conceal the strength of their first three starting cards. Knowing the order in which players received their cards is a key requirement in reading their hands. It's just my personal opinion but I believe rearranging the order of your upcards goes against the spirit of the game and should not be allowed.

Fortunately, this is not an issue when you're playing online or in a cardroom.

ONE PAIR ON FOURTH STREET

If you started with a small pair and did not make two pair or trips on fourth street, then you need to have picked up a straight or flush draw to continue playing

This is one of the most common and costly errors that most stud players make. If you start with 3♠ 3♦ Q♣ and get the 7♥ on fourth street, you have missed and you should fold. In this example, you needed a queen or a 3 to continue playing.

Your fourth street card is very important.

—fold

—fold

But, if you get fourth street cards like these—

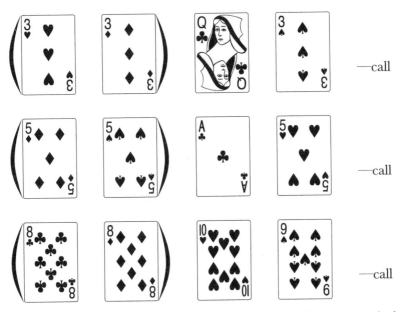

—call

—call

—call

The 9♠ adds sixteen more outs to your hand (the sixes, sevens, jacks and queens).

(4♦ 4♥) 6♣ 5♠—call. The 5♠ add sixteen more outs to your hand (the twos, threes, sevens and eights).

If you have a pair and a three-straight or a three-flush (or both) to go with it, it's usually correct to look at one or two more cards

That is, if conditions permit. If the betting is light, your cards are high, live and you can win if you make your hand (you're not drawing dead), then it is correct to take another card.

This brings up a well known but infrequently-seen-in-print concept regarding seven-card stud: It is correct to chase cards to make one of your multiple possible hands. For example, you have (A♦K♣) 10♦K♦. Any diamond, ace, king, queen, jack, 10, or even 9 will improve your hand. That's 22 out of 46 unseen cards that will improve your hand on the next card alone. And you still have sixth and seventh streets after that to possibly improve.

These types of hands are very common at seven-card stud and you should almost always play them until the end because—and I'm about to give away a big seventh street secret ahead of time—when heads-up on the end, it's correct to call with any hand that can beat a total bluff. That means that your big pairs will be useful as bluff catchers at the end of the hand. You also have the added advantage of having the best pair when an opponent checks his pair of sixes and you check your pair of kings.

Play any single pair that is higher than your opponents' suspected two pair

With more cards to come, you have a better chance of improving than he does and you will often both have two pair on sixth street. If you have (A♥A♣) J♠8♠ on fourth street and an opponent has an obvious two pair of queens-up, you will often have the higher two pair by sixth street. Don't forget to look around and see if the cards you both need are live.

RULE OF THUMB

The hand that you can see is always a favorite over your opponent's possible better hand.

This means:

Your one pair is a favorite over his possible two pair.

Your two pair is a favorite over his possible trips.

Your trips are a favorite over his possible straight.

Your small straight is a favorite over his possible higher straight.

Your flush is a favorite over his possible full house.

This rule of thumb means that it's okay to call with a weaker hand than the one you fear you're calling.

If you have (J♦J♠) X and your opponent catches a jack, it probably did not help him

This concept holds true for all ranks of cards. I just used jacks as an example. A possible exception might be an ace because an ace-high straight or flush draw is a good hand to have.

The 8♥ probably did not help Player A.

If you started with a straight or a flush draw and totally miss getting any help on fourth street, you should usually fold

This is a common occurrence and it is one of the biggest and most costly mistakes that beginners and long-time players make. If you start with three hearts and get a club on fourth street, your odds of making the flush just went way down. That means that two of your next three cards must be exactly of the suit you name—and that's hard to do. Unless that club allowed you to pick up a quality straight draw, the correct move most of the time is to check and fold. I know that sounds like incredibly tight play, but knowing the odds makes it an easy play.

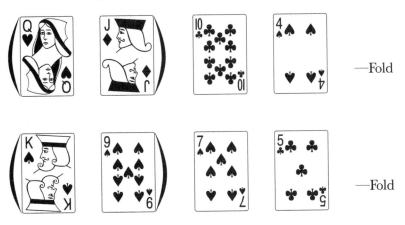

—Fold

—Fold

Fold unless you don't have to call a bet.

If you start with a three-flush and miss your flush card on fourth street, the odds of making your flush just went down from about 50% to about 20%.

With three cards to come, two of the three cards to be drawn must be of your suit and the odds against it are about 25-1.

Your best strategy is to eliminate players and possibly win the pot right there.

That's assuming you're reading the other hands correctly and your one pair is the highest hand in the game right now. Players with two small pair will often correctly fold. The players on straight and flush draws have only four cards and you should make them pay do draw against your hand. A-A is 50-50 against a single opponent with a four-flush and a slight 53-47 favorite against an ace with a straight draw. A-A is a big underdog against two or more of these draws at the same time. Be willing to bet with just one pair on fourth street. You will often actually have the best hand at that point and you still have opportunities to improve.

(A♥ K♠) A♠ 9♦ is even money against (J♠ 10♣) 9♠ 8♥ but is still a very strong hand worth betting against one player.

If your pair is the two smallest cards you have, you should look for every reason to fold

I know it's easy to call with a pair of fours with the thought, "If I catch another 4, I'll have trips and they'll be very well concealed. You won't catch another 4 often enough to make it worth drawing to. You'll lose a lot of money with these types of hands and when you do get the 4 and win the hand, you won't win back all those bets you spent on other hands where you missed and lost. Learn to check and fold when you have a small pair.

This is a folding hand even if both of the remaining fours are live. The doubled bet on fifth, sixth and seventh streets just makes it an unprofitable hand to play.

Realize that other players will bet with nothing on fourth street

Wow, is this ever so true in home games. Many times the bettor on fourth street will have only a straight or a flush draw. He might be betting because he's counting on making the hand, he thinks you might fold, or he's trying to get you to check on the next round, when the bets double. Be willing to call with just one pair, if you think you have some way to win the hand.

Call if...

You've got the bettor beat in sight and there's a reasonable chance he could have a worse hand than yours.

You should often raise with what you know are second-best hands on fourth street

That's because you:

1. Can still improve to a better hand;
2. Might have misread the situation and actually have the best hand at this point;
3. Get in a raise with a winning hand;
4. Induce players to check to you on the next round, when the bets double.

When you both check on fifth street, you've saved 1/2 of a bet and they've lost 1/2 of a bet that they could have had if they knew you were going to check.

You have

Raise if you're looking at

If he has two pair, you are still a favorite to finish the hand with a better two pair.

YOUR DOOR CARD IS PAIRED ON FOURTH STREET

As a reminder, the bets don't normally double until fifth street. However, if there's an open pair showing on fourth street, you have the option making the single or the double bet. This is true for all the players in the game on fourth street ; you don't have to be the one holding the open pair to make the double bet.

In the board below, any one of the six players in the game can make the doubled bet. But that does not mean you have to. If you're playing $5/$10 limit and player B is first, he can bet either $5 or $10. If he bets only $5, any other player can raise $10 and from that point on, all bets and raises must be in $10 increments.

YOU:

A:

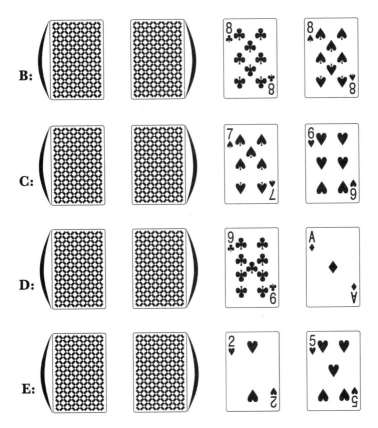

You can bet double, but a single bet looks suspicious

If you made high trips, you're probably going to win the hand. Bet double if you think they'll call any size bet anyway. A single bet might be necessary if they're a little conservative and you want a sure call.

is probably going to win the hand, especially with live cards. You just have to use your judgment as to how to make the most money in the hand.

Hands like

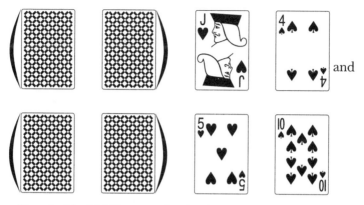

will probably fold if you make the doubled bet. But hands like

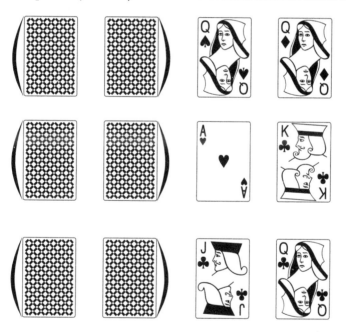

will probably call if you make the doubled bet. Look around and give it some thought when deciding which bet to make.

You should bet double to eliminate players with straight and flush draws

Players with straight and flush draws have only four cards at this point and obviously need at least one more card to make their hands. This is where you can really punish them for trying to draw out against you. Make them pay double if that's the hand you put them on.

is a big favorite over hands like

and

You can't make them fold but you can charge them for their attempt to draw out on you. Might as well make it a big bet.

You should bet for value when you have the best hand

Getting a lot of money in the pot and then winning that pot when you have the best hand is the essence of all forms of poker and all the different poker games. If you think you're going to win the hand, make that pot as big as possible. Keep in mind, however, that that strategy sometimes calls for you to make the smaller bet here rather than the big bet.

You should bet small when you have a lock

Unless you think they'll call a big bet anyway. This is where you get into "…they think you think they think you think…." Presumably, you know something about the other players and you have an idea of their calling standards. The point is, don't automatically make one bet or the other all the time. Put some thought into it and let the game conditions help guide you.

If you have

and your only opponents has

you might want to consider making the small bet. Better to have him call $5 with a losing hand than have him fold when you make a $10 bet. Make the big bet only if you're very certain he has some reason to call.

Beware of other players who have also paired their doorcards. If an opponent started with a pair, there's a two out of three chance that he just made trips

Don't get so excited over your own good fortune that you forget you're still in the middle of a poker game that you have to win. Look around. Pay attention. Be alert. Slow down for a second if you have to. If you and another player both just made trips on fourth street, and you have the higher trips, you are about a 10-1 favorite to beat him. But be aware that another player could beat both of you.

Is there a higher pair than yours showing?

This is the flip side of the above advice. You could be the one who is the 10-1 underdog. This is an area where expert and very experienced players can lay their hands down on fifth or seventh street. Try to remember those times you made low trips and lost the hand. See if there's a way that, in hindsight of course, you could have seen it coming.

If two players both make an open pair on fourth street, it's about 9-1 in favor that at least one of them made trips.

If

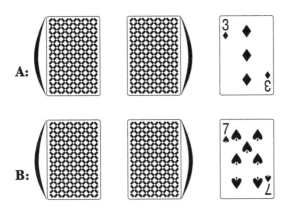

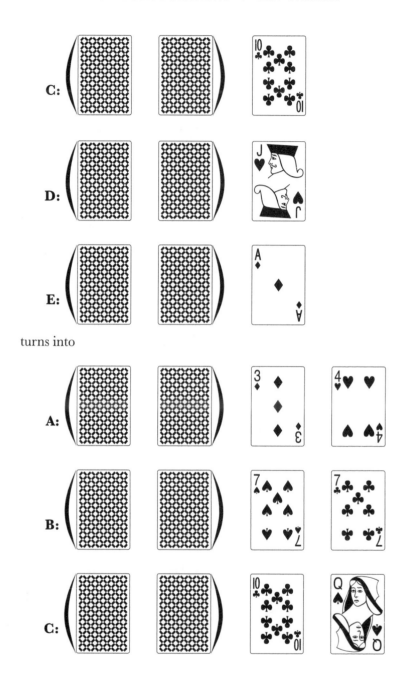

turns into

then it's about 90 percent certain that either Player B or D now has trips.

If two or more players paired their door cards, then it is statistically likely and probable that at least one of them has made trips

That's because the two cards that they started with that you can't see aren't just any two random cards. One or both of those hole cards has a strong relationship with the door card. Very often the player's door card will be part of the pair. Naturally, when he duplicates that card, he now has trips.

You just can't fight the math on this one. You need to watch both of these players closely for signs that you're beat. When reading their hands, especially on seventh street, you can afford to err on the side of giving them more credit for a good hand, rather than less. Be more inclined to think you're looking at a full house rather than two pair or trips, especially if he's played it like a full house.

Look for your opponents' door cards to be dead in another player's hand

If you're looking at (XX) Q♣ Q♥ in another player's hand and you remember that the Q♦ was folded on third street and you have the Q♠ buried in your hand, then you are in a very powerful spot. Let him represent trips if he wants to. The information you have reduces the possibility that you will make a mistake when playing against him.

Don't underestimate the value of remembering cards that have been folded. And if you do, keep it to yourself! You might think it's difficult to remember folded cards (it's easy with practice) but you should at least get into the habit of remembering folded cards that affect your hands. If your first three cards are all diamonds, then you should be counting folded diamonds and looking for them in the other player's hands.

Consider check-raising to get more money into the pot

When the pot is huge and there are a lot of players involved, forget about deception and just do whatever it takes to win. As the pot gets bigger and bigger, it will become more and more obvious what your hand is anyway. Who cares? Either they're going to credit you with a good hand and fold, or more likely they'll call all the way to the end. They'll either pay you off in a failed attempt to beat you or they'll knowingly pay you off with a losing hand simply because the pot is huge and they can beat a bluff on the end. You can't always control what's going on in their minds so just build a big pot and then win it.

TWO PAIR ON FOURTH STREET

Once you make a great hand on fourth street, say two big pair (aces and kings), your strategy changes from wanting to get players out to wanting to keep them in.

Your chances of winning the hand just shot way up, especially with three more cards to come. With a big hand on fourth street you can now tolerate having a lot of players in the hand trying to draw out on you. This becomes truer as there are fewer cards yet to come.

These are the types of hands that can win without further improvement. Start thinking about how to maximize your profit.

Keeping the above advice in mind, you do want to raise to get the stragglers out when you have the two big pair

But this is a double-edged sword. Many times there will be stragglers who can't hurt you. They will have horrible hands with no chance of winning because they're drawing dead. You really want these types of players to call all the way because you're going to win the pot. But you can never be sure if they're truly drawing dead. This is where experience comes in. You can start to gain this type of experience just by taking the first step—and that is to just be aware that these types of hands exist.

- Two pair is more vulnerable to a drawing hand than trips are. To improve two pair, you must get exactly one of the four remaining cards of your pairs.
- To improve trips, you only need to pair any card in your hand.

If you have a hand that needs protecting, players who missed what they were hoping for on fourth street usually need to be eliminated. A raise from you will take care of that.

Two small pair is much worse than they look

They will fill up (make full houses) only 12 percent of the time from here if, and only if, all four of your cards are live. Also, they cannot beat most other two pairs. Most good players actually fold if they make two small pair on fourth street and there's a bet due them.

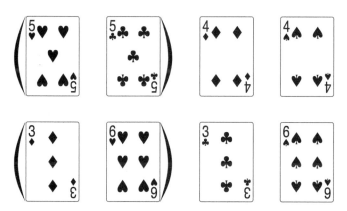

The small pairs above are all much worse than they look. Do not be overly impressed because you just moved up the poker scale of hands from one pair to two pair. This is usually the end of the upward mobility of these hands.

If you make an open pair on fourth street and it gives you trips, you should usually not go for the check-raise

Even though it's a good idea to bet for value and try to build the pot, it gives away your hand too soon. Your hand will be too easy to read and that kills your action. You should wait until fifth street to check-raise. The pot will be big, the other players will be more committed to calling anyway because they only need two more cards, and the bets double on fifth street.

If you have

and you bet right out, you might have just one pair, two pair or trips. But if you check-raise your opponents will easily and correctly put you on trips. This could kill the action you could have gotten from them on fifth, sixth and seventh streets.

You do not always need the best hand to bet

If you have any kind of hand at all and there's a chance that you could eliminate players or win the pot right there you should not give any free cards. Betting on fourth street can actually be a defensive (rather than offensive) move because it might induce everyone to check to you on fifth street where the bets have doubled.

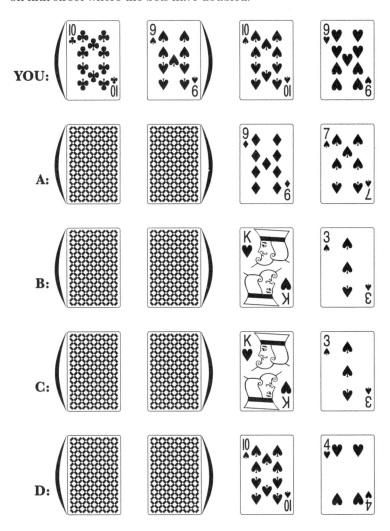

If you raise against the above hands without the best hand at this point, you might get a free card on fifth street and you still might improve on fifth street. You have two ways to win—make them fold and improve your hand.

Your success comes from being able to read the other players' hands

It might be right to raise in one situation and fold in another with the same two pair. Since the median winning hand in seven-card stud is three nines, then the median losing hand might be a high two pair. You have to be able to read hands and apply situational common sense. You can win and lose a lot of money with the exact same hand—it's the other players that makes the difference.

You are a 3-1 underdog against trips on fourth street

This is why it's so important to be able to put other players on a hand. Look for their cards in other players' hands. Two pair has only four outs to make a full house while a hand with trips only has to pair any other card in the hand.

is a 3-1 underdog to

Be more inclined to call if your two pair is concealed

This brings to mind one of the fundamental elements of poker—it induces the other players to make mistakes when playing against you because they will have misread your hand. You will be able to get in extra bets with winning hands because they won't be sure of what you have.

is a much more powerful and profitable hand than

because the strength of your hand is concealed. It's the same hand but the arrangement of the cards makes all the difference. Having the open pair chills the betting action because your opponents naturally won't bet into a hand better than theirs. If you're bet into when you hold an open pair of queens, it usually means that the bettor has you beat.

Most raises made on fourth street are made by players holding two pair more than any other hand

Since two pair is the most common high hand after four cards, that just makes sense.

You should usually only raise or fold with two pair on fourth street

Exactly what you do depends on what your two pair are, what hands your opponents likely have and how the betting is going. To paraphrase Shakespeare, "Two pair is not two pair is not two pair." You should raise and call all raises with

but check and fold with

Both hands are two pair, but as you can see, they have very different values.

TRIPS ON FOURTH STREET

This is a little different from the previous category describing how to play when you pair your door card. That's because, in case you forgot, pairing your door card does not automatically mean you made trips. In the eyes of your opponents, it's a maybe/maybe not situation. What happens when you definitely make trips on fourth street?

You're the only one who knows it for sure

This gives you some latitude in how you choose to play the hand. You can slowplay, check-raise or do whatever else it takes to win the hand. It gives you a chance to evaluate all of the game variables up to this point and make your best educated decision—from a position of strength, of course.

If you have

you're in a very powerful position because, in the minds of your opponents, you could have any one of the following hands:

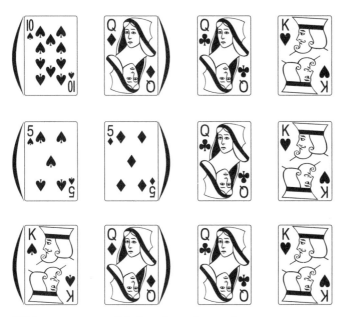

With so many possible hands to choose from, your opponents will rarely correctly put you on the actual hand you have.

FOUR OF A KIND ON FOURTH STREET

What a problem to have! It's 270,724-1 to make quads in four cards. My advice is to play quads like you would play trips with the knowledge that you are going to win the hand. If you're really lucky, and it does happen, I hope you're playing seven-card stud in a casino poker room and you lose this hand. In that case, you'll win the bad beat jackpot!

If you have

       or

or

in your first four cards, you just beat 270,724-1 odds!

FOURTH STREET REVIEW

- Do you have the best hand at this point? If not, who does?
- Are your cards live?
- Did fourth street kill some of your outs?
- Do you have a quality, winning draw?
- Are there any useless cards in your hand? Why?
- Did you pick up a backdoor straight or flush draw? How many more outs did it give you?

Remember, two pair will improve to a full house only 20 percent of the time by seventh street. If you have high trips, you will probably win the hand.

Do not play all four-straight draws. If you're going for a gutshot, all four cards have to be live. Just two dead cards means you can't profitably play the hand.

A four-flush will make a flush by seventh street only 47 percent of the time. Subtract 5 percent for every dead flush card you see in someone else's hand.

If you have top pair in sight and are raised, you should fold. That is, if you're showing A-A, K-K or Q-Q and you're raised by a player who's not even showing a pair, you should fold.

Get ready for fifth street. All bets from here to the end of the hand will be double bets. It will cost twice as much, or more, to play out the rest of the hand from here than it cost to play the hand this far. You should be willing to fold often on fourth street simply because that is usually the right play on fourth street.

FIFTH STREET STRATEGY

Fifth street is the time to fold if you don't have the best hand or a draw to the best hand

You might have made a loose call on fourth street when you missed but now the bets have doubled. If you missed on two cards in a row, this is the time to get out. It is a point of no return. If you call on fifth street it should be with the idea and commitment that you are prepared to go all the way to seventh street. If you're playing correctly and you have the hand you should have by now, it's no problem staying around for the last card.

It's never too late to fold when it's clearly the best move

It is wrong to call on fifth street and then fold on sixth street. However, if you realize that you made a serious mistake by calling on fifth street, do not compound that blunder by calling on sixth street when you know you should be folding.

Call on fifth street for the right reasons

Do not call just because you've put a lot of money into the pot up to this point. Your call should be based on your estimation of your opponents' hands and your relative strength, coupled with a knowledge of outs and pot odds. Don't throw away money trying to protect a bad hand.

It's hard to fold on fifth street

It sure is. Who wants to fold a five-card hand when you need to see only two more cards? Yet, this is what separates the winners from the losers. You have to learn to recognize those times when you can't win the hand in any way and it's going to cost you a lot if you don't get out.

On the other hand, fifth street is the time to bet and raise to eliminate stragglers, small pairs, busted draws and weak hands

You're a definite favorite against any one of these bad hands alone. The problem is that you're not a favorite against all of them collectively at the same time. So you can't let too many players in the pot if you have the best hand. Raise.

When you've made a hand on fifth street that you're sure will win the hand on seventh street, you might want to wait until sixth street to raise

If you're sure that it won't hurt you to give everyone another card, you can wait to trap them for an extra bet. Let other players have a chance to draw dead against you. Give them a chance to make their straights and flushes if you're holding a full house. Since they also might know fifth street is the time to fold bad hands, you might let them stay in for one more card, and they will usually (incorrectly) call a raise on sixth street because they need to see only one more card. Also, the more players you allow to play, the more likely it is that one of them will make a hand that will be able to raise or reraise you on a future round of betting. If you drive opponents out now, that won't happen.

If you make

on fifth street, it would be a shame to bet and have everyone fold right there. If that happens, then it's your own fault for not reading them properly and seeing that they can't call a bet. You might want to consider checking, letting one of them be the bettor and check-raising only if you're sure you won't lose one of them. Otherwise you want to build the pot while playing passively.

Let everyone get to where "I just need one more card" before you lower the hammer on them. Key concept: Most players who take a sixth card will almost always call all bets and raises just so they can find out if they make their hand on seventh street.

If you have the second-best hand, it is often correct to raise if you believe it will get you heads-up with the best hand

This improves your chances of winning the pot because you now have to beat only one player instead of two or three.

If there are five players each with the following chances of winning the hand

A	B	C	D	YOU
40%	20%	15%	15%	10%

and your raise will eliminate three of them, then your chances of winning the pot might look like this:

A	YOU
60%	40%

40 percent is a lot better than 10 percent.

Remember, a straight is the lowest ranking of the completed hands

If you have a straight on fifth street and someone else makes a flush, higher straight, or full house or better by seventh street, you may not win the hand. For this reason you should try to win the hand right here if it looks like you're facing any other drawing hands. The only straight I really like is the ace-high straight because it takes a flush or better to beat it. I don't like making a straight only to lose to another straight.

YOU HAVE ONE PAIR ON FIFTH STREET

A common seven-card stud question is, "How do you play one pair on fifth street?" That's a good question because it's such a common situation and the cost of misplaying the hand is high. Here's a list of things to think about:

1. Do not automatically fold. Fold only because you think you're beat and can't win the hand by seventh street.

2. If your opponent has two pair, then your pair has to be higher than both of his. This is so that when you improve, you will have the higher two pair or trips.

3. Look for your live cards. If you have A♣ A♥ K♣ 9♦ 7♣, then you're looking for the other kings, nines and sevens.

4. Do not play one pair on fifth street against more than one other player, unless you can play for free.

5. This is the hand you will have 75 percent of the time on fifth street. Since it's so common you should consider the possibility that this is often what the other players also have. Don't automatically assume you're beat, especially if there are no pairs showing on board.

A high pair on fifth street can usually be a calling hand if you haven't picked up obvious signs of strength.

YOU HAVE TWO PAIR ON FIFTH STREET

The most important factor is how live your cards are
You only have two more cards to draw and at most you'll have only four outs. Can the two pair you have now win a showdown on seventh street? The second most important factor here is how big is your two pair?

Two pair is a very difficult hand to play
Sometimes, you should muck in one situation and raise in another—with the exact same two pair! The difference depends on your opponents' upcards, their probable hands, an accounting of the live and dead cards, and how the betting is going. This is the hand and the street that separates the winners from the losers. Unfortunately, the best way to learn how to win is to have lots of experience, and that experience comes from losing.

If you have

against

you should raise! Your higher cards give you a good chance to finish with the better hand. However, if you have that same

against

you should fold. Your opponent's higher cards means he has the better chance to finish with the best hand.

New pairs on board

A player who makes an open pair by pairing his fourth street card (not the door card) will more likely have two pair rather than trips. You should always watch for players who get new open pairs on the board, even as late as fifth and sixth streets.

A player who has

will most likely have two pair. But what if his board were arranged like this:

Now, he very likely has trips, even though he caught the same card on fifth street.

YOU HAVE TRIPS ON FIFTH STREET

Look for your live cards

You're in the enviable position of having to pair any card in your hand to improve to a full house, rather than drawing to just one of four specific cards as with two pair. If you have three kings and you see your other king in another player's hand, I want you to know that that's not totally bad. Of course, it completely eliminates the possibility of making four of a kind but it improves your chances of making a full house.

Bet

You will almost always have the best hand at this point, even if you're looking at an opponent's scary board. Trips are always a favorite against possible trips. Back off only if you're given a clear sign that you're beat. Be on the lookout for someone who does have you beat but is slowplaying until sixth street.

Against three flush cards showing

The obvious implication is that the player has a five-card flush. Your trips are always a favorite against a possible five-card flush and you still have two more cards with which to possibly improve. Your opponent most likely has a four-flush. Don't let him draw for free. He will usually call a bet on fifth and sixth streets only to miss his draw on seventh street.

A player showing

almost always does not have the flush. But that doesn't mean he can't make one by seventh street.

Know the opposition

A lot of players will play loose and bet, raise and reraise just to be in action and build a pot. However, if the tightest player at the table raises and reraises you, you're beat.

YOU HAVE A STRAIGHT ON FIFTH STREET

Try to win the hand right there

A straight is the lowest of the complete hands. Any player who makes a straight or any other completed hand will likely beat you. You'd like the hand to be over right there. The only good straight, in my opinion, is the ace-high straight because it takes a flush or better to beat it. Start to look around for possible higher straights in the making.

YOU HAVE A FLUSH ON FIFTH STREET

Bet for value

Expect to be paid off handsomely if you win the hand. No one believes that you'll have a flush in five cards. They will usually assume you have a four-flush and are betting on the come.

If you have

you will get a lot of action because in the minds of your opponents, you could have

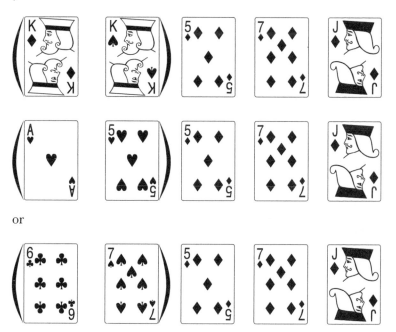

or

You can always bet against someone having a flush in five cards—unless they have one! Of course, this only applies when it's you who has the five-card flush.

YOU HAVE A FULL HOUSE ON FIFTH STREET

Let them catch up

You've now reached the point in the hand where you want them in the hand, donating to this pot that you're going to win, rather than folding and letting you win a small pot.

If you have

you might want to consider checking so the other players can catch up with you. They will call with second-best hands but they often need six cards to get there. Sometimes that six-card second-best hand will be a draw that needs a seventh card.

Watch for higher pairs on board than yours

If your full house is Q-Q-Q-9-9, you should be very worried if another player makes an open pair of kings. The reason is obvious, especially since he played this far against you with the cards you have showing. He must have had something, and a split, hidden pair of kings is my first guess.

If you have

be wary if another player is showing

Even if he doesn't yet have the kings-full full house, he has a good chance to make one by seventh street.

YOU HAVE FOUR OF A KIND ON FIFTH STREET

Since it's a cinch you're going to win the hand, you need to use your poker sense to play this hand in a way that wins you the biggest possible pot. Usually, all you have to do is play it like you have a good full house.

For those times when you have the monster hand on fifth street, you should resist making extra bets and raises that may not be called. Bet all that you think will be called and not a chip more. Let opponents take that sixth card on the next round and then you can hammer them. They'll call for sure because, after all, they only need one more card after that to see if they make their hands.

If you have

your strategy changes from one of trying to win the hand to one of maximizing the profit in a hand you know you're going to win.

YOU HAVE A STRAIGHT AND/OR A FLUSH DRAW ON FIFTH STREET

1. Calling is not automatic. Your cards have to be live and you have to believe you'll win the hand if you make the draw.

2. You cannot call two or three bets cold. With that kind of betting going on in front of you, you're being told (in poker lingo) that you're already beat and drawing dead.

3. If you can see, or have seen in folded hands, a total of six or more of your flush cards, you have an easy fold. That's unless you also have a live straight draw that you really believe will win if you make it.

4. You should fold open-ended straight draws if three or more of your straight cards are dead.

5. Be wary of players who catch a straight card on fifth street that is also the same suit as their door card. This might mean that they now have a four-flush.

6. If fifth street gives you a four-flush and an overpair, you have a very good hand. You now have a little insurance against missing your flush draw and you now have a small chance to finish with two pair or trips.

SIXTH STREET STRATEGY

You should play fifth and sixth street together in a nearly identical manner

The biggest difference, however, is that you will have more information with which to play sixth street than you did fifth street. This is the time to review the above notes on fifth street Strategy because you need to combine them with the sixth street strategy. Everything that applied on fifth street also applies to sixth street.

If you take a sixth street card, it should be with the idea that you're going to almost always take a seventh street card also

By this time you'll have either a very good hand or a quality draw that will win the hand if you hit it. The pot will usually be big. If you are truly undecided about whether to play or not, it's because your hand is probably a genuinely borderline hand for the situation you're in. If the pot is huge, tend to call. If the pot is small, tend to fold.

The odds of improving with one card to come are:

Two pair	11-1	against
Trips	4-1	against

Four-straight or a four-flush draw: It depends on how many total up-cards you've seen and how many of the cards you need are dead. The odds are usually about 4- or 5-1 against.

If you have a good, but vulnerable hand, your goal is to eliminate players, rather than let them stay in the hand

Good hands win but vulnerable hands often lose. See if you can get those players with two pair, straight and flush draws to fold. You're a favorite over any one of them when it's just the two of you, but you're a huge underdog to all of them together at the same time.

Do not give free cards when you have any reasonable chance to win the pot on seventh street

An obvious exception is if you know your opponents are drawing dead. If you really can't decide what you want your opponent to do, it's much better to have him fold right there than it is to give him a chance to hit a miracle card to beat you.

Make the players who are still on straight and flush draws pay

If you have a high flush or a full house you will make more money in the hand if you can get players with losing hands to put money in the pot. Don't check so they can make their hands for free. Bet because they will call you anyway.

Realize that no one will fold on sixth street; everyone will usually call your raises

If you made a monster on fifth street and were holding back, now's the time to let it out. Most players will now call your raises because they need to see only one more card. And who folds when they need only one more card?

You should occasionally raise on sixth street if you know you intend to call on seventh street

If you can see that you're going to finish out the hand with a bet on both sixth and seventh streets, you might want to occasionally put both of those bets in at the same time on sixth street. This has several advantages.

1. It might make someone fold who would have beat you on seventh street if you hadn't raised.
2. You might win the pot right there.
3. Everyone might then check to you on seventh street because you showed obvious strength on the previous betting round.
4. If you improve to an even better hand, or still have the best hand, you can bet again on seventh street with the satisfying knowledge that you got in an extra bet with a winning hand.
5. And if something changes on seventh street and you need to check, it might not cost you any more than the two bets.

The most common hand you'll have at this point is two pair

Remember, you will improve to a full house only 1 time in 11, and that's only if all of your cards are live.

Once you make a completed hand (a straight or higher) look for solid reasons to fold

I'm not advising you to try to make a straight just so you can fold it on the next round. What I'm saying is just be on the lookout that some-one could make a better hand after you make yours. You should fold only when it's obvious that you won't be able to win the hand. Once the average player makes a straight or higher, it never crosses his mind that he should sometimes lay it down. Don't be that average player. It's never too late to save a bet or two if you think it's the right thing to do, regardless of what's happened previously in the hand.

> **Don't be afraid to make a solid, thoughtful laydown on sixth street when it's obvious you're beat and/or drawing dead.**

Threatening-looking boards are often empty threats

It's statistically rare that a player will hit perfect-perfect-perfect to make exactly the hand he needs to go with his first three cards. A player whose board is representing a straight or flush often has just one pair. You'll have to look around for his live cards and make an educated guess as to what he has. This player will often check on seventh street if you called his obvious strength on sixth street.

Your hand will have either obvious, visible strength or your strength will be concealed

Think about what you think the other players think you have. They will base their actions largely on what they think you have. If you look weak, they will bet. If you look strong and they bet anyway, look out. Figure out how to make the most money you can. Consider check-raising as a tactic to build the pot but don't check with the intention of slowplaying.

Bet if you have a strong looking board

Give opponents a chance to respect your strength and possibly fold. Bet your strong hands but realize that if you bet in this spot with noth-ing, you'll probably be called anyway simply because it's sixth street and it would be right for them to call you. Think ahead. Are you going to like it if you bluff on sixth street, get called, and then have to bluff again on seventh street?

Calling raises

It's not the amount of the raise you should be worried about so much as the fact that another player thinks his hand is good enough to raise with while he's got you and the original raiser to think about. A raise on sixth street is almost always a bet for value. The raiser usually expects to win the hand.

Beware of raising wars between two other players

If two or more other players are raising and reraising you should be aware that one of them is definitely not bluffing. This is especially true if either or both of them have open pairs showing. This is often a sign of a full house-full house or full house-versus-trips battle. A player with no pair showing is signaling obvious hidden strength if he raises a player with a pair showing. If the player with the pair showing raises then you know you're looking at two big hands.

Raises and reraises from unexpected sources

If a player with a weak board showing reraises, and it's totally unexpected based on the way he's played the hand up 'till now, you can be sure he has the best possible hand he could have at this point. If he doesn't have a pair showing, he's got a big flush.

Check-raising

If you check with the intention of raising, and then no one bets (they all check after you), you can be sure you have a winner at this point. This means that you can bet slightly weaker hands than usual on seventh street. The fact that they all checked is a tell.

Who has a full house?

You must have a pair showing by sixth street to have a possible full house. Try it. Remove five full house cards from a deck, add a sixth odd card and then try to arrange them two down and four up without having a pair showing. It can't be done.

Position is important

If there are a lot of players in the hand and the first bettor is on your immediate right, you should usually just call with monster hands. Do not raise and drive them all out, even though they should call if they're playing correctly. Call in the hopes that one of those many players after you will raise after you call.

Your position will not change after sixth street

Up 'till sixth street your position in the betting order could change with every new card because there could be a new high hand with every card. However, the position you're in on sixth street will also be your position on seventh street. How do you feel about that? Are you trapped between two raisers? Do you like it or would you rather fold because you know you're going to have to call a lot of big bets on sixth and seventh streets?

Usually call with anything against only one player if the pot is big

If you are heads-up on the river, you should realize that it will be difficult for either one of you to bluff the other out of the hand. It's correct for either one of you to call the other with almost any bluff-catching hand. Conversely, don't try to bluff out a single opponent at this stage of the game.

If you do decide to bluff...

I guess no advice is written in stone. Sometimes you will feel like a bluff might work, even when your opponents has to call only one bet to keep you from stealing a big pot from him. This most important factor that will help you pull off this bluff is your upcards. If your board looks legitimately powerful you can often get good players to lay down one big pair. But, be warned: That same player will usually correctly call you with two pair.

> **Sixth street is the time to raise, check-raise, get in extra bets and do whatever you can to build the pot if you have the winning hand.**

SEVENTH STREET STRATEGY

By the time you've come this far, your hand will play itself

Your best guiding principle is to play direct, straightforward and uncomplicated, even if it makes you feel like you're giving your hand away. You should bet when you have the best hand, raise if you think it will win you more bets and call if you think that will win you more bets.

Forget about bluffing, for the most part

Unless you have some very specific reason to think that a bluff attempt will work, you should usually just check and fold if there's a bet. That's because most players will call you with anything in this game, just to see what you have.

If you have a good hand, do not bet into what you think is a busted straight or flush draw

Since this player cannot call a bet on the end—the last card—you won't win any more money when you bet. You should check to a player who you think has a busted straight or flush with your good hand. There is the chance that he will try to bluff you. If he bets, you've got an extra bet in the pot from him that you could not get in there if you had bet first. At this point there is no harm in raising because now he will either call or fold.

If you check first, hoping to induce him to bluff, and then he checks right behind you, you do not have to feel bad about it. That's because he could not have called your bet anyway and you have not lost anything.

A check-raise on seventh street is rarely a bluff

The check-raiser knows you won't fold and let that big pot go for lack of calling one last bet. When you call him he will have the goods.

Who was on a draw?

Take the time to watch the players who you think needed that last card to make their straights and flushes. Watch how they react when they look at their seventh street card. Some players who were on a big draw or needed a card to win a big pot will often let you know they missed right away. They might act disgusted, throw their cards, curse, fold out of turn or even turn their cards up for all to see as they fold them. The key is, you need to pause a moment to give them time to do this.

Remember the dead cards

If you're a good player, and you're trying to win at this game, then you should have been paying attention during the play of the hand. That means you should have been keeping track of the cards that get folded along the way, especially the third street cards at the beginning of the hand. This will help a lot of you know a player needed a folded card to make his hand.

Don't go on automatic pilot

Don't make the easiest, most obvious play every time. Take the time to think and figure out how to get the most money into the pot, or drive another player out of the hand or whatever your goal is. Sometimes, there's more than one way to accomplish your goal.

Unexpected raises

A player who has a terrible looking board, who hasn't made a move during the entire hand and who you expected to fold suddenly raises and reraises on seventh street almost always has a perfectly hidden full house. That's just the way it is.

If a player showing

suddenly and unexpectedly starts raising and reraising, expect him to have a perfectly hidden full house almost every time.

Reading your hand

At the showdown, if you think you have any chance at all to win the hand, you should always turn all of your cards face up on the table. Take the time to carefully figure it out. If you are a beginner, you will sometimes find that you unknowingly backdoored a hand you weren't looking to make.

STRATEGY SUMMARY

The key to winning at seven-card stud is simply to start with the best hand or a draw to the best hand and then to protect and improve that hand as the game progresses.

If you are not a winner at seven-card stud, there's a good chance it's because you're not aware of the above advice. Perhaps you are ignoring or deliberately violating some of the above guidelines. Chances are, you have the typical beginner's weakness of needing to "see just one more card." If this is you, then stop that! I can tell you that that strategy has already been tried by millions of players and it has conclusively been proven that it doesn't work.

There is no need for you to try to reinvent the wheel. All you have to do is periodically review the above strategy guidelines and follow them as best you can. The only acceptable reasons for losing a hand at seven-card stud are either you didn't make your draw that would have won the hand or you had the winning hand going into the last round and someone drew out on you. If you're losing for any other reason (other than being cheated) all you have to do is follow the above strategy advice to turn that around.

19 MORE STRATEGY TIPS

The following advice will help clarify some of the strategy guidelines mentioned in this section. This will make the game a lot easier and more fun to play.

1. The single most important decision that you will make in any poker game is whether or not to call that first bet. You don't have a lot to lose when you don't have anything invested in the hand. A bad decision here will usually cause you to chase your money and your draws when you should not have even played to begin with. For some players, a decision to call that first bet automatically means they will call all the other bets as well.

2. You not only have to remember what cards everyone called the initial bet with, you have to remember which cards were folded at the beginning of the hand. It's really helpful when you see an open pair in someone's hand and you remember that both of the other cards of that rank were seen and then folded.

3. There are two advantages to having a lot of players in the hand. This first applies to all forms of poker: if you win the hand, you will win a bigger pot. The second advantage applies only to stud. The more players that receive upcards, the easier it is for you to determine how many outs you have and to know if your cards are live or not. If two players play to fourth street, then you will only see eight upcards. If six players play to fourth street, you will see twenty-four upcards. That makes computations more accurate.

4. A raise on third street usually means the raiser has a split pair. That means he has a pair of whatever his door card is. In the absence of any other information, this is what you should take his hand to be until you can determine otherwise.

5. A player who reraises on third street usually has exactly what it looks like he should have. If he has (X X) A♦ you can be sure it's a pair of aces. Don't overlook the possibility that he could have rolled-up trips. Even though it's statistically unlikely (424-1) that anyone will be rolled-up on any one hand, a player who reraises is more likely than that to have it.

6. A big pair played heads-up against a single player with a straight or a flush draw is a favorite to win the hand.

7. A player on fourth street or later who pairs his third street card is very likely to have made trips. That's because two out of three pairs on third street will be split pairs.

8. A player who pairs his fourth street card more likely has two pair or just the one open pair instead of trips.

9. You cannot make a straight or a flush in four cards. So, that's the time to make the straight and flush draws pay to beat you. They don't have a hand yet and they're going to have to pay for the privilege of drawing.

10. It is not profitable to draw to a straight when another player is obviously drawing to a flush. There are four possible outcomes in this situation:
    a. You miss/he misses
    b. You miss/he hits
    c. You hit/he misses
    d. You hit/he hits

    Of the four possibilities, only one is good for you, and not consistently good at that. That's because you won't always win the hand when you make your straight.

    Your hand is better when two players are obviously drawing to a flush in the same suit. The worst case scenario is when two or three players are all trying to make a flush in different suits while you're drawing to a straight.

11. The weaker your hand is or the more vulnerable it is, the happier you should be to win the pot early. Do not be disappointed if you win just a small pot before all the cards are out.

12. If you are on a draw, think about how you can win the hand if you miss the draw, because that's what's going to happen most of the time. That's why it's good to always start with high cards because this gives you the option of pairing them if you don't make the draw.

13. A player who raises or reraises on sixth street with a pair showing almost always has a full house. Ask yourself if this player would play his hand like that if all he had was trips or two pair. Most of the time the answer is, "No."

14. If you have two pair on sixth street, you will not make a full house on the end eleven out of twelve times. And that's if all four of your outs are live. That's why you need to start with high pairs.

15. When the action begins on seventh street, you should recall who had to make the bring-in bet on third street. You'd be surprised to see how much this helps you read his hand by seventh street.

16. A player who raises and reraises strongly on seventh street with no apparent straight or flush draw almost always has a perfectly hidden full house. If his board is (X X) K♥ 9♠ 7♦ 3♣ (X) and he obviously really likes it, it's a full house. This is a good time to try to account for his out cards.

17. A player who makes a flush will usually make it in the suit of his door card, which is the first upcard. That's because most flush draws start out with two or three cards to the flush. It's mathematically difficult to start with two spades and a diamond and end up with a diamond flush—but it happens.

18. When two players have the same hand or the same type of hand, who wins? Often, both players will have been on a draw and they both missed. The pot usually goes to the more aggressive player who made the last bet.

19. If you play seven-card stud in a public poker room, you should try to move up in limit as soon as possible. Do not let the slightly higher limit intimidate you. You are more than compensated by the fact that the players are a little better and therefore easier to read. They usually play the cards they're supposed to play, they play the way they're supposed to, and they often have the hand you think they do. Also, the rake is a smaller percentage of the pot and this increases your profits.

RAZZ

Razz is simply seven-card stud played for low. That is, the lowest hand, instead of the highest hand, wins the pot. The object of the game is to finish with five cards that are lower than anyone else's five lowest cards. The value of your hand is know by it's fifth lowest card. For example, if your five lowest cards are A-2-4-7-8 then you would say you have an 8 low.

A♠ 2♦ 3♣ 4♥ 5♠ is a 5-high straight but when you're playing razz it's also known as a **wheel** and it's the best possible low hand you can make. The fact that's it's also a straight is not a factor because straights and flushes are not recognized hands in razz and they do not count against you in the way that they count for you in traditional seven-card stud.

A♦ 2♦ 3♦ 4♦ 5♦ is a straight flush but when playing razz, again, it is simply a wheel. The fact that it's also a flush, and a straight flush at that, is meaningless. Again, straight and flushes are not poker hands in razz.

A♦ 2♣ 3♥ 4♠ 6♣ is called a 6-4 and is the second-best hand you can make in razz.

A hand consisting of A♥ 3♣ 5♦ 7♠ 9♥ J♦ K♣ is a "9 low," because the fifth-lowest card in the hand is the 9♥. If another player also has a 9 low then the tie is broken by the next-lowest card in the hand. In this example, the player's hand is a 9-7. If the other player has a 9-8, he loses to the 9-7, but if he has a 9-6, 9-5 or a 9-4, he wins.

If both players have a 9-7 for low then the tie is broken by the third-lowest card in each player's hand. Whoever has the lower card wins. This tie-breaking procedure continues through all five cards, if need be. If all five cards are identical in both players' hands, then the hand is a tie and the pot is split.

Remember that the hand's value is know by it's fifth-highest card. 4♦ 5♣ 6♦ 7♠ 8♥ beats A♥ 2♦ 3♠ 4♣ 9♣ for low even though at first the latter hand looks better because of the four wheel cards.

OVERVIEW OF RAZZ

WHY PLAY RAZZ?

You should learn to play razz because so many of the poker games you'll be playing in private home games are played high-low split. That means the highest poker hand splits the pot with the lowest poker hand. Razz has it's own special techniques and strategies that don't apply when you play the same game for high. The player who can learn how to play expert poker for low and then integrate that ability with what he knows about playing for high, will have a huge advantage in high-low split games.

HOW DO YOU PLAY RAZZ?

The hands are dealt exactly as they are in seven-card stud. In fact, this is a seven-card stud game where the only big difference is that you're trying to make a different kind of poker hand. Here's how the game is dealt:

1. Each player antes before the cards are dealt. If you're following my advice mentioned at the beginning of this book, the dealer will make the ante bet for all of the players.
2. Each player is dealt two downcards and one upcard.
3. The highest card showing is forced to make the minimum bring-in bet. If there's a tie for the highest card, then the tie is settled by suit. Most casinos and public poker rooms use reverse alphabetical order of the suits—spades, hearts, diamonds and clubs (♠, ♥, ♦, ♣) to break the tie for the bring-in

bet only. This is the only time in razz where the suits of the cards are a factor.

4. From this point on, the game is dealt just like traditional seven-card stud except that, starting on fourth street, the lowest hand showing bets first.

5. A-2-3-4-5 is the lowest possible hand. Think of your ace as a 1-count card. It is the lowest card you can have.

6. Straights and flushes do not count as a high hand or any other type of hand. You should pretend that straights and flushes don't exist because they don't mean anything in razz. However, there will be rare times when both you and your opponent finish with two pair or trips. Sometimes you both might have to play two paired cards in your five-card hand. Lowest pair wins.

7. There is no qualifier in razz as there is in some high-low split games. The only real qualification, if you're looking for one, is that you finish the hand with a better low than your opponents. If you have any trouble at all trying to figure out who has the best lowest hand, all you have to do is arrange the hands in order from highest to lowest, as in traditional seven-card stud. The lowest hand wins.

8. There are no jokers or wild cards in razz. If that's the type of game you want to play, then you should take a look at the chapter, "Popular Home Games," later in this book where you'll find plenty of suitable candidates.

What are some of the more attractive characteristics of a razz game?
Since you're all trying to make only one poker hand, you don't have to spend a lot of your mental energy trying to figure out if your opponent has made a straight, flush or a full house. Remembering dead cards is still important but not as critical as it is in seven-card stud. Dead cards are a good thing in razz while they're a bad thing in stud. That's because each dead card you can see is one less card in the deck that can pair you up, which is something you don't want.

If you have

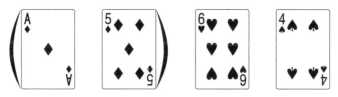

you're a lot happier if you look around and see

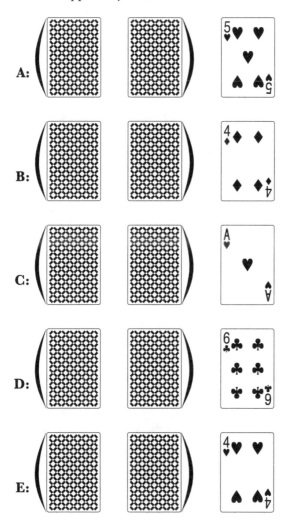

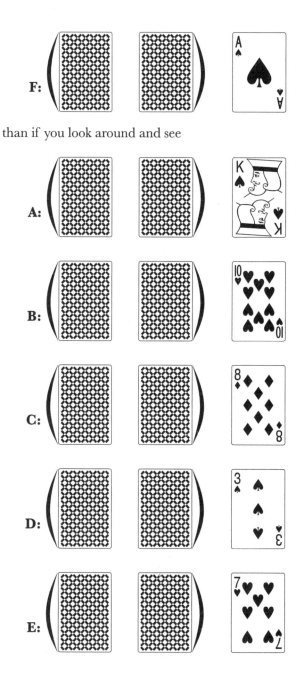

F:

than if you look around and see

A:

B:

C:

D:

E:

F:

The aces, fours, fives and sixes that you see in the other players' hands means that the cards you need to improve your hand are still live.

When you see players playing with the 8♦, 3♠, 7♥ and 2♦, it implies that they have other low cards to go with it. That means that some of the cards in your hand are also in their hands, which is good for you.

Reading hands is still important but is made a lot easier because players will fold their bad hands more often. Most hands, when the game is played correctly by experienced players, are played only two- or three-handed, even when eight players are dealt in at the beginning. Betting and calling decisions are easier to make, as well as decisions on how to handle bluffing on the last card.

However, don't be fooled. As you're about to find out, playing for low has it's own complications and difficulties that most recreational players aren't aware of. There are many special situations and conditions that apply to razz that don't apply to regular stud. The players who understand these things the best will be the biggest winners at razz and most high-low split games.

THIRD STREET STRATEGY

Just as in almost all other poker games you'll ever play, the most important decision to be made is the decision to even play at all. A decision to call that first bet is often the most costly decision of all. That's because, once you've entered the pot, you'll usually play the rest of the hand incorrectly. And that's expensive. I just described the truth for about 95 percent of all poker players. Let me teach you how to become one of those other 5 percent of players.

Stealing the antes

The first thing that should happen after the first three cards are out is that everyone should be looking for an opportunity to raise in an attempt to steal the antes. Why? Because you know ahead of time that only one or two other players will have playable hands. Chances are you won't be called a lot of the time. You will often win the pot right there, which is why you should try to steal more often when the pot is small compared to the bet.

When you are called, the caller's hand will be very good and therefore easy to read, which gives you an edge. You could have anything but you know the caller's hand is good.

When should you try to steal the pot on third street?

1. When you have a three-card 8 or 9.

2. When you have two low cards and your highest card is hidden.

3. Anytime you can see that, based on the other player's up-cards, you won't be called.

Fold if you are reraised and your hand has a 10 or a facecard. This is the time to let it go. You made an attempt to win the pot and it's clear that you're beat. Don't send good money after bad. You were caught stealing and the best thing you can do is wait for the next hand.

If you try to steal the antes with

and you are raised, you will almost never have the best hand at this point and you should fold.

Never try to steal with only one low card, even if it looks like you won't be called. You have two factors working against you:

1. You might be called anyway.
2. You don't have, and won't finish with, the best hand.

Never try to steal when you hold a hand like

Your two bad cards coupled with the chance that you might be called by even one player makes it a very unprofitable play. Just fold when you're dealt two high cards.

Don't try to steal the antes with your very good hands. Steal with A-2-9 but not with A-2-5. Why? It's because you'll win a lot more money with the A-2-5 if you let players in to play against you all the way to the last card. You can win either the antes right now or a big pot in a minute or two. Your choice.

Do you see the subtle difference between the two above hands?

When there are many low cards showing on third street

The first thing that's true is that, on average, there are a lot high cards hidden face down in the other players' hands. Also, it is very likely that two or more players will be playing this hand. Therefore your cards have to be better than they would if only one player was playing. You can beat one player with a mediocre low hand but you need a great starting low to beat two or three more players.

> From this point on, I'll use "L" to indicate low cards (8 or smaller) that help the hand in the example, and I'll use a "W" to indicate a wheel card (A, 2, 3, 4, or 5). That's because it's not important that a low card be any specific card as long as it helps make the five-card low.

(LL) 9♦ is a playable hand against only one player but you need (LL) 8♣ to play against two other players, and you need a smooth 8 or a (LL) 7 to play against three more players.

It just makes sense that you need better hands to beat more players.

Where do you stand on third street?

One way to answer that question is to compare your door card with everyone else's. If you have a wheel card, or even a 6 showing, you have options, as you will see. A low card showing makes for a possible good starting hand. Another way to look at the question is to know where you stand in relation to the other upcards. Ordinarily, a 9 on third street is not representing a very good looking hand. However, if you look around and see that you've been called by a jack, a queen and a king (it happens in wild home games), then you all of a sudden have a good hand.

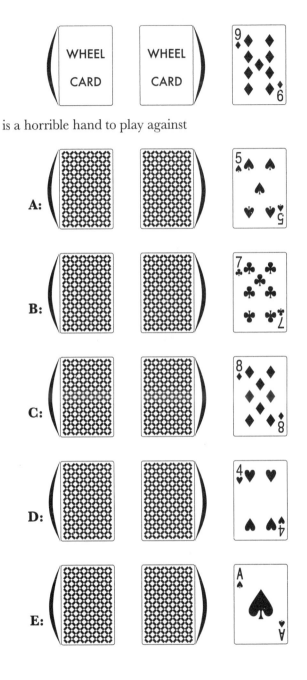

is a horrible hand to play against

but is a great hand to play against

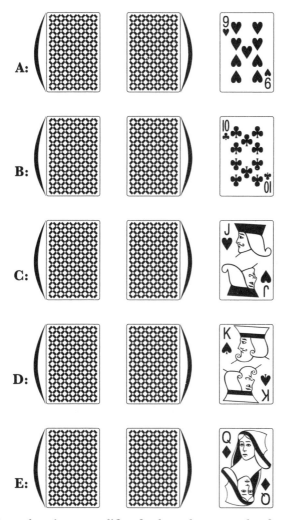

Since there's no qualifier for low, the strength of your hand is relative. When you see that you have a three-card 9, your fist reaction is that you have a bad hand. But, when you look around and see your opponent's upcards, you'll realize that you have a good hand after all.

To draw an analogy from blackjack, the object of the game is not to get as close as you can to 21 without busting. It is to beat the dealer. What you do often depends largely on what his upcard is. Sometimes you will take a card because of the dealer's upcard and sometimes you will stand because the dealer has a different upcard. It works the same way in razz.

If you're going to play on third street ...

It should be because your other two downcards are live and good. Think about what the other players might have, especially the good players. A good player who voluntarily calls with a 7 or 8 showing almost always has two wheel cards in the hole. That means that if he catches a 6 or 7 on fourth street, it most likely improved his hand and did not pair him. Alternatively, that also means that a 2, 3 or 4 on fourth street might have paired him.

A player showing

probably has two good hole cards and probably improved his hand if he makes

but he might have paired up if he makes

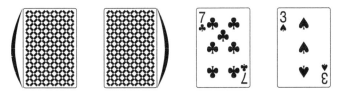

or one of the other wheel cards on fourth street. You'll never know for sure at this point but it's something to think about.

The other cards showing are important, even if they're folded

If you start with A-4-7 and you look around the board and you see two more aces, a 4 and a 7, then that dramatically reduces the chances that you'll be paired up on the next round or two. If you see a lot of twos, threes and fives, then you know that your chances of catching these cards just went way down. When you combine these two lines of logic and you see aces, fours and sevens but you don't see any twos, threes, fives or sixes, then you have a great hand. The cards you don't want have been removed from the deck and the cards you do want remain.

This is why, given the specific cards that are out, a higher starting hand can be a favorite over a lower starting hand in the long run.

If you have

you have a good chance of improving if you look around and see

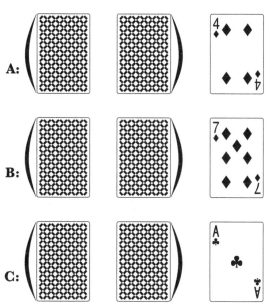

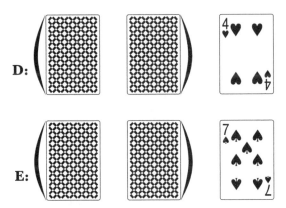

but you have terrible prospects of improving if you see the following:

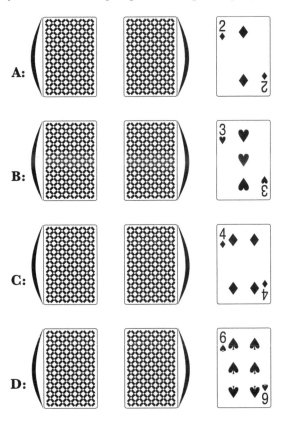

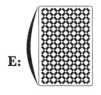

E:

Is your highest card also your upcard?

You're the only one who knows the answer to this question. This is important because you'll have to learn to think ahead. The other players will play according to what cards you're showing them. Hidden strength is worth more that obvious strength. With several players, (XX) 8 ("X" being low cards) is usually a fold hand because, with four more cards to come, you won't finish with the best hand. However, if those cards are arranged as (X8) X, you have options. You might draw a strong looking board and if you pair your 8, you won't always have to fold, and it might stop a bluff on the end.

If you have

and catch the 8♣ on fourth street, it will look like it improved your hand to an 8 low. However, if your opponents knew that you now have a pair of eights, it would be same as if you held

and you lose your ability to represent a good hand. The arrangement of the same four cards makes all the difference in the value of your hand.

You must learn the difference between 'rough' and 'smooth.'

Rough and smooth are terms that describe the strength of your hands in terms of what your second-best cards are. This is very important because most winning hands will be a 7 or 8 low. In cases like this, it's the second best card that breaks the tie. And sometimes it even comes down to the third or fourth card. Many times, when you announce at the end of the hand, "I have an 8," and your opponent says, "So do I," you will lose the hand. Why? Because you had a rough 8 and he had a smooth 8.

Rough means that your second card is high and **smooth** means that your second card is low. 8-7-6-3-2 is a *rough* 8 while 8-4-3-2-A is a *smooth* 8. Whenever you see that you might tie with another player, you need to start figuring out which of you have the smoothest draw. The analogy from seven-card stud is when both you and your opponent have four-flushes of different suits showing on board. Suddenly, a flush is no good. It has to be a *high* flush.

> L-L-L-7-8 is a rough 8.
>
> A-2-3-4-8 is a smooth 8.
>
> L-L-L-6-7 is a rough 7.
>
> A-2-3-4-7 is a smooth 7.

Three-card 9's are usually no good

However, there are exceptions.

1. If you're heads-up.
2. If the pot is not raised on third street.
3. Of course, when you can see that you have the lowest card showing. But as I just pointed out above, your other two cards have to be very good. You need a smooth 9. Think ahead. If you never played a three-card 9 you would probably be slightly ahead of the game. As a general guideline and rule of thumb, this is the dividing line between playable and unplayable hands.

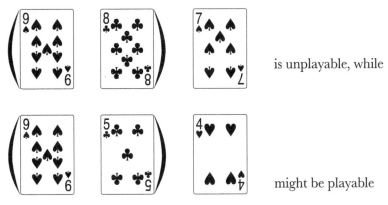

is unplayable, while

might be playable

When you start talking about making an 8, 9 or 10 for low, you have to start giving serious thought to what your second-lowest card is going to be. The need for a tie-breaker in razz is common.

When you have only one bad card...

You should never play against more than one player. This is a simple rule and you should be able to remember it. One other player might also have a bad card, and then you'd have a chance. But you can't beat two players with one bad card. You need three good cards to start.

It's a seven card game

When you play with a bad card, or even two, then you are really playing with only five or six cards when everyone else will be playing with seven. You can sometimes play with one bad card in stud because you can sometimes use that card to help make a flush or a full house, but that same bad card in razz will needlessly use up your quota of seven good cards. You cannot play six-card poker and win when everyone else is playing seven-card poker. Most of your starting hands have to be three good cards.

An advanced concept

Most players will call on fourth street and beyond when it is incorrect for them to do so. However, if the pot is really big after third street, it often becomes correct for them to call with those same bad hands. Hands that were an obvious fold now become worth calling with to see one more card. A bigger pot makes it more correct to play looser, call more, chase more, see more cards and stay 'til the end. Keep the pot small if you have a decent, but vulnerable hand. If it's wrong for them to chase you, and they do, then you win in the long run. Don't make it correct for them to chase when you would rather they didn't.

Remember, this advice applies when you have a decent, but vulnerable hand. If you have an awesome three-card starting hand, go ahead and build that pot, because it's wrong for them to try to run you down.

It's wrong for a player to chase you down when he holds

when the pot or small or contains only the antes, but it's correct for him to play this hand when the pot is big.

Memorize your hole cards!
Memorize your hole cards. A player who draws a new card on future rounds, and then double-checks his hole cards, is announcing, "I just paired up!" Don't be that player unless of course you're deliberately sending a false tell. For those of you who do take this advice, an additional reward is that you don't have to remember suits.

If you have a problem with this, you should at least try to remember the cards that were folded on third street.

This will often come in handy on seventh street.

What's the biggest difference on third street between razz and seven-card stud?
If you call the initial bet in seven-card stud, it is often correct to do so with the idea that the time to fold will be fifth street if you have to. If you then call on fifth street, it's with the intention of playing through seventh street. You will rarely call on fifth street and then fold on sixth street. That's because you might start with a decent hand and then pick up a straight draw and then a flush draw or two pair or trips by fifth street.

You'll often have the right cards and pot odds to then see the sixth and seventh cards. If you can't make a full house then you might win with trips. If you can't make a flush then you might win with a straight.

This is absolutely not the case in razz! The time to fold in razz is on third street. That's because many of the reasons that you would call in stud just don't exist in razz. There are no other better types of hands that you can make to win if you can't make a low draw. You just can't say, "I can beat your wheel because I've got a …". There just is no other hand than a low hand in razz.

When you can tell just from looking at your first three cards that you won't be able to steal the blinds, you don't have the best hand and you don't figure to finish with the best hand, you just have to fold on third street.

So, what is the biggest difference between seven-card stud and razz? It's wrong to chase past third street in razz.

The only hand you're trying to make in razz is a low hand so you either must start with three low cards, or at least three cards lower than the other players.

FOURTH STREET STRATEGY

The Golden Rule of Fourth Street Strategy

If you started with three good cards and catch a bad card while your opponent catches a good card—fold. Yes, I said fold. Cut it off right there. The pot is small and you are now playing with only six cards while he is playing seven-card poker. You don't mathematically figure to catch up by the river and the pot is not offering you the right odds to continue with the hand. Since his hand is low, it will be up to him to bet first, and he will always bet his better-looking board into yours. You're playing a guessing game from here and that's not the way to play winning poker. Experts with years' of experience say this is the best move in this spot and sure enough, computer simulations have proved they are right.

You would almost never make this move in stud and that's what make's it so hard to do in this stud-like game. Just remember: this game is played for low and everything is turned on its head. This rule is so important that you'll be a winner even if you ignore the rest of the fourth street strategy advice presented here. That's because this mistake occurs so often and costs so much that all of the other fourth street mistakes can't begin to make up for it.

If you have

and your opponent also has a good-looking low like

and you catch

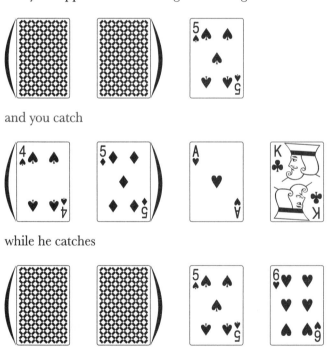

while he catches

you should fold.

Here it is again: If you both start with three good cards and he catches good when you catch bad—fold.

You pair one of your hole cards

The fact that you will have a good-looking board will compensate you for that fact. Pairing your hole card is not the same thing a catching a bad card, as talked about in the golden rule of fourth street strategy, above. This difference is in what your opponent sees. If he sees you have (XX) 6 3 (and you have a 3 in the hole) he will have to play and call with better hands than he would if he was looking at your (XX) 6 Q. You should check and call if it won't be too obvious that you're doing so because you've paired up. Otherwise, go ahead and bet because your board may run him off and you'll win right there.

If you have

and catch another 2 or 4, you still have a playable hand.

A Seventh Street Tip Revealed Here on Fourth Street

"You will win much more than your fair share of hands if your four upcards look very good.

You will win a lot more hands when you have

than you will if you have those same cards arranged like this:

Four low cards in stud could mean any hand from one pair to a full house but in razz they can mean only one thing—a low hand. Take advantage of that fact and use your good-looking board to your advantage when practical.

When you know you have the best hand

You should realize that your opponent will also know you have the best hand and it will be correct for him to fold if you bet. So, you should occasionally check and call with what you know is the best hand. This will put doubt in his mind about your hand. He will probably think you paired up and it might induce him to misplay his hand on future rounds. This is doubly good for you because the bets will be double after this round. He will be betting and calling on future rounds when a bet from you on fourth street would have told him he should be folding. Sacrifice that one small bet on fourth street so you can win double bets on fifth, sixth and seventh streets.

If you have

and your cards are live, you might want to think about checking and let them catch up—but you don't have to! Act like you have a pair of fives if you think it'll make you more money in the long run.

When you have a mediocre hand

You might be able to tolerate a cheap showdown against one player but you can't afford to pay to try to beat two or more players. It takes a much better hand to win against two or more players than it does just one player. Razz is a game of good starting hands and just one high card takes you out of the running against several players. Like I said earlier, it's not like you can make some other hand if you miss your low draw.

might win against one other player but not two or more players unless they check, thereby indicating you just might have the best hand at this point.

You have four cards to a 7 or better

You have just beat big odds and you should almost always play to the last card. You are a prohibitive favorite against just one other player and you're a big favorite against two other players. Start putting in the raises even if you miss on fifth street. Problems begin when three players can see your board and they're playing anyway. Look out.

If you have

or any other 7 low, you are better than 50-50 to make a 7 low or better.

FIFTH STREET STRATEGY

Now you know what they have

Well, not exactly, but you do know one thing—a player with three cards showing has to play one of them in his final five-card poker hand. You can discard two cards at the end but not three. The lowest card showing in a player's hand is the best hand he can ever end up with at this point.

A player showing

(in five cards can end up at best with only an 8 for low. An easy way to see this is to pretend he has two perfect cards in the hole and his next two (and last) cards will also be perfect for him. This is good to know when you're trying to make a smooth 8 or better. Also, don't forget to give him credit for two very good cards in the hole at this point since he voluntarily called an initial bet with a 9♣ showing.

A draw can be much better that an already-made hand

Five points:

1. Smooth draws to low cards are always favorites over 8- and 9-low hands at this point. A player who has A-2-3-4-K has two more chances to catch a 5, 6, 7, 8 or 9 to beat an already-made 9. That's two draws at one of 19 cards. If he makes a hand as bad as a 9 low, he will beat all other nines because he will have a smooth 9 against a rough 9.

2. A four-card 5 or 6 is a favorite against a made 9.

3. A made 8 is a favorite over any four wheel cards. The problem with playing against the wheel draw is that you won't know if another wheel card on sixth street paired him up or not.

4. Two face cards showing are always unplayable. You have only two more cards to come and you have to hit perfect-perfect.

5. Not only do the last two cards have to help your hand, but they can't pair you up. This has to happen at the same time

you're making a better hand than your opponents. It's no good to try to hit perfect-perfect to make a 9 low while your opponent obviously has an 8 low or better.

Razz is a game of strong-looking boards

Take advantage of that fact. A slight hidden weakness is not always that bad for you. Remember that half the deck is made up of high cards and there's a good chance that most players have one of two of them. Bet your good-looking boards because you can win by making everyone fold and you still have a chance to make a good hand.

You can win with this queen-low hand

but you can't win with this queen low:

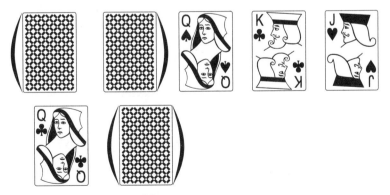

Appearances are everything.

SIXTH STREET STRATEGY

If you take a card on sixth street

It should be because you have a good hand and the two cards you'll get on sixth and seventh street have a good chance to improve your hand. If you call on sixth street you should usually go ahead and call on seventh street. Don't do this because you're following a blind strategy as you would be in seven-card stud. Do it because your hand, your opponents' hands, and the pot odds justify it.

Fold on sixth street if...

1. You made a really bad or questionable call on fifth street and you catch a bad sixth street card. No need to compound a mistake with stupidity; or

2. Everyone caught miracle cards to drastically change the situation (and their boards) and you can now clearly see you're beat.

If you called on fifth street with

and catch a bad card on sixth street —fold.

Does your opponent have a hidden pair on sixth street?

1. If he started with three wheel cards and has three low cards showing—it's about 50-50 he has a hidden pair.

2. If he started with three wheel cards and now has four low cards showing—it's a little more than 2-1 that he *does* have a pair. Somewhat humorously (I think, anyway) it's about 1 in 5 that he now has two pair. This is speaking from a purely mathematical point of view. It's up to you to look around and see if his cards are live or dead.

3. Even considering 1 and 2 above, he still has a great hand to draw to.

4. If he started with cards slightly higher than all wheel cards, and all wheel cards are now showing in his hand, he undoubtedly already has made an excellent low hand.

A player showing

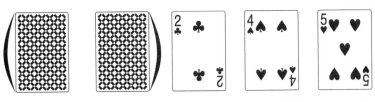

has about a 50-50 chance of having a hidden pair of fives. Remember the basic poker odds that says about one-half of all poker hands are a pair or better? This is true because one of his two hole cards is very likely to be another 5.

A player showing

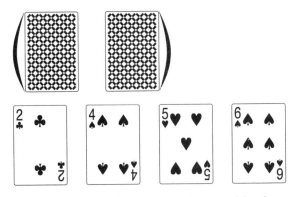

has about a 20 percent chance of having two pair. But this does not necessarily mean that he has a bad hand. He still has a very good hand to draw to with one more card to come.

Always bet on sixth street if...

1. You think your opponent will fold and you *need* him to. In other words, bet with what you know is the worst hand but your opponent thinks is the best hand. Or, in still other words, bet when you think your opponent has you beat, but he can't call because of your board.

2. You know you will win the hand but your opponent doesn't. Bet if you have a 4-card low board like

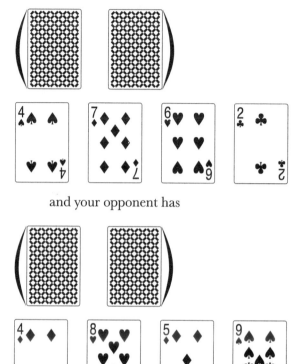

and your opponent has

regardless what your other two downcards are. This advice, of course, assumes that you've played the hand this far with two good hole cards.

Always check on sixth street if...

You know you're going to win the hand but your opponent won't call if you bet now. If you check now and let him have a 7th card, he might improve his hand a little and call you on seventh street. He might also call on seventh street because a bet from you might be a bluff in his mind. After all, you would have bet on sixth street with a hand and he might think you now have no option but to try to bluff the hand on seventh street.

If you have

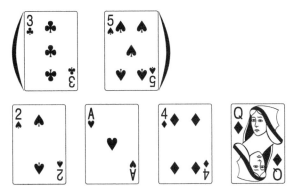

you should check if you know your opponent can't call. This would also apply if you had a made 6-4 low. Bet on seventh street. He'll call with almost any hand and any other hand that can beat a total bluff.

SEVENTH STREET STRATEGY

Always figure out your opponents' best possible hand
This is obvious advice but it doesn't hurt to remind you. Sometimes the excitement of playing the hand will cause you to overlook something once in a while. And, it's hard to play every hand perfectly every time. A player showing K-3-8-9 can, at best, have only an 8 for low.

> **Easy read:**
>
> **Your opponent's best hand can only be what's left of his hand after you discount his two highest upcards.**

can *at best* be only a 7 low.

can *at best* be only a 10 low.

Any player showing two wheel cards can have a wheel, but his three hole cards have to be perfect, including that last, seventh street card. He could also have a 6-4, which for all practical purposes, is just as good as a wheel.

Always call on seventh street if...

Your opponent' board cards forced him to bet first during the hand. In this case, he didn't necessarily bet because he had the best hand—he was forced to bet. Chances are, he's got hidden weakness.

You started with an obvious good draw and a player bets a possible 9, 10 or jack into you. You should call. The reason is, is that he should be afraid of your good draw. And if he, indeed, does have a 9, 10 or jack, he should check it. He should then call as a bluff-catcher. This bet is usually a bluff.

A player showing

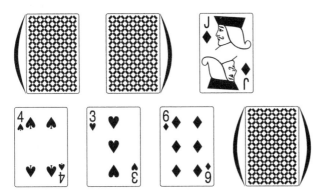

probably did not want to play the hand if he was forced to make the bring-in bet.

Made hands are favorites over possible hands

A made 7 is a favorite over a *possible 6* and a made 8 is a favorite over a *possible 7*. Unless you have superior hand-reading skills and you know better, in most cases you can profitably call these possible hands. Don't forget that there are twenty nines, tens, jacks, queens and kings in the deck. They have to be somewhere.

Tie-breakers

Realize that many times it will take the second-best and sometimes even the third-best cards to break a tie. When two players both have a 7 low, the next-highest card determines the winner. If you're new to razz and the concept of low hands, there is a little trick that you can perform to help determine the lowest hand. All you have to do, given the five lowest cards that a player has, is determine who has the highest hand. That's easy. He loses.

Close calls

Sometimes your opponents' board will look a lot like four of the seven cards that you're holding. In this case it's possible that your hands are very close together in strength. You might have a winner but if you check you might lose a bet you could have won if you had the confidence to bet your hand. All you have to do is figure out which two or three cards he must have in the hole. Then think about how likely it is that he has them, given the action, the betting, the exposed cards and your summary of the situation. You can usually bet against him having *exactly* what he needs in the hole.

Bluffing is common on seventh street because it works

If you bluff on the river in seven-card stud, it's correct for your opponent to make a crying call with a hand as weak as a pair of aces. That's not the case in razz because you will only bluff on the river in razz when your board supports the likelihood that you have the hand you're representing combined with the board that your opponent is showing.

Raise only when...

You're certain your opponent will call with a worse hand. For this to work, you have to have a certain winner and he has to have a good second-best hand. He won't call a raise with any other hand.

Ken Warren's best razz tip

Don't play razz! That's right, I said don't play razz. What I'd like you to do is become an expert at razz, and then incorporate it into other games so that you're playing a high-low split game. That's because razz is a relatively boring game but the razz expert can win a lot of money if he can play it while also playing another game. The most common high-low split game, and the most obvious application of this tip is seven-card stud high-low split with or without a qualifier for low.

Not by coincidence, that's the subject of the next chapter.

SEVEN-CARD STUD HIGH-LOW SPLIT

Well, this ought to be easy. All you have to do is read the chapter on seven-card stud, add that knowledge to what's in the chapter on razz and *voila!*—you're a seven-card stud high-low split player. Right? Wrong! As you're about to find out, whenever you combine two games you're not just playing two different games at once, you're playing an entirely new third game. This means that you have to know the strategy for three separate games all at the same time. Fortunately, you already have a good head start if you've read the previous two chapters.

OVERVIEW

What is seven-card stud high-low split?
Seven-card stud high-low split is the standard game of seven-card stud with one very important difference. That is, you are also playing the game of razz (seven-card stud for low) at the same time with the same cards. You are free to play for high only, or low only or both high and low at the same time. At the end of the game, the highest hand splits the pot with the lowest hand. If two or more players have the same high or low hand, then they split their half of the pot between them.

Why play seven-card stud high-low split?
Seven-card stud high-low split is among the most popular home games. Also, if you know how to play this variation, you will have an edge

when playing other home games that are similar to stud and played for both high and low. And there are a lot of them. Check out the chapter on "Home Poker Games" immediately following this chapter. Texas hold'em might be the most popular casino poker game, but if you play in a home game, you're going to be playing a lot of high-low split stud games and a lot of variations of it.

There's another reason to play this game and it applies to the good players. Seven-card stud is a very difficult game to play correctly. It takes a lot of knowledge and skill to be a winner. There are many opportunities to make costly mistakes. The same is true of razz. The player who can master both of these games will be a big winner at high-low split because the average player just doesn't have a clue. You should play this game because of the advantage that a good player has over weaker players.

How do you play seven-card stud high-low split?

1. Home games are usually played with an **8 qualifier** for low. That is, the highest of your five lowest cards cannot be higher than an 8. If your hand is A-3-5-6-8, then you qualify to win low and you will win unless another player has a better low hand. If your hand is A-2-4-6-9, then your hand is known by the highest card, which is a 9, and you don't qualify to win low. The player with the highest hand would win the entire pot if no other player has a qualifying low hand.

2. You can use all of your cards to make your highest and lowest hands if you're going to play for high and low at the same time. A typical two-way hand would be 2-3-4-5-6, which is a 6 low and a 6-high straight for high. Another common two-way hand would be A-2-4-5-8 of all one suit. That would be an 8 for low and a flush for high. If you had both the highest and lowest hands you would win the whole pot.

It's important that you understand this from the beginning. This means that you can use any five of your seven cards to make your best high hand. Then, after you've done that, you start all over and you can use your best five of seven cards to make a low hand. The fact that you may have used one or two of your cards in your high hand to help make a low hand is of no consequence. It doesn't matter. They're all your cards. You can use any cards you choose to make a high hand and you may use any of those same seven cards to make a low hand.

If your seven cards are

then your high hand will be

and your low hand will be

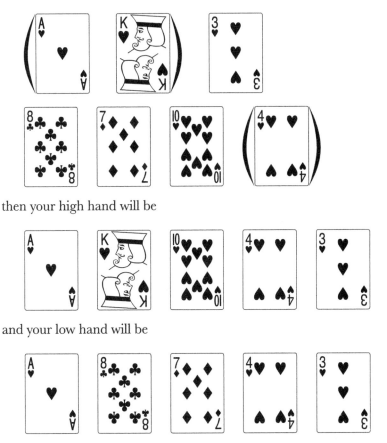

As you can see, you've used the A♥ and the 3♥ in both your high and low hand.

3. Aces can be used for both high and low. If your cards are A-3-5-7-8-A-3, then you would have an 8 for low and two pair—aces and threes for high.

If your hand is

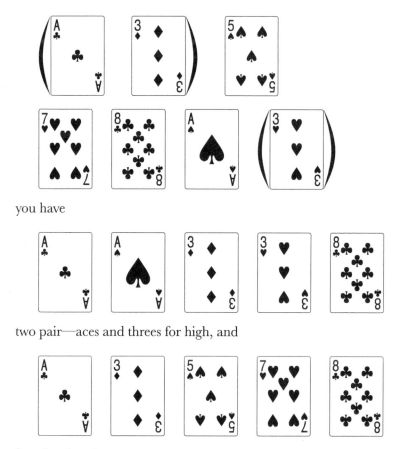

you have

two pair—aces and threes for high, and

for a low hand.

4. The highest card makes the initial bring-in bet. In home games, the players decide whether it's the highest or lowest board showing that makes the bets on fourth street and beyond.

5. This game can be played as either cards speak or declare. This is how you decide which direction each player is going at the end of the hand. In **cards speak**, every player turns his hand face up at the showdown. The best hands win the two halves of the pot, if there's a **qualifying low** hand—five unpaired cards 8 and below. If no hand qualifies for low, then the highest hand wins the whole pot.

In **declare**, the players declare which way they're going (which half of the pot they intend to contest) and then they compare hands. They do this by concealing chips or coins in their hands and then opening their hands simultaneously. Players who have one chip in their hand are declaring low. Two chips is a declaration for high and three chips is for both high and low, which is called **swinging**. All of the players who declared low compare their hands and the lowest hand gets half of the pot. The players who declared high do the same. This is where skill at reading hands, trickery, deception and common sense come into play.

Declare adds an extra element of skill to the game. That's because your hand does not have to support your declaration. If you're the only one who declared high or low, then you're an automatic winner for half the pot. Players who have low hands can declare high if they think they will be the only one to do so. A player might have a great-looking low board but actually have two pair and a king for low.

Some home game players like to have another round of betting after the declare but before the cards are shown. After the declare you know who you're competing against for your half of the pot. If you're the only one to declare high or low, and several other players all declared in the opposite direction, then you're in a really sweet spot.

Declare works best if you're playing with no qualifier for low, because it allows the better players (that's you) more freedom to manipulate and deceive their opponents. You can go low with any hand if you figure all the other players for high. It also encourages bad play from opponents right from the beginning because they'll always be thinking, "Well, if I don't make my high hand I can always declare for low." Sure they can. And you'll be there waiting for them with a better hand.

You need to add the words 'scoop' and 'freeroll' to your vocabulary

Good players usually only play hands that have a chance to win both the high and low sides of the pot. This is called **scooping**. A freeroll is when you've made a good high or low winning hand and you have a chance to make the other half with more cards to come. A 6-5-4-2-A for low with four hearts is a good example of a freeroll hand. You've already got the low hand locked up and a 3 or a heart will make a straight or a flush for high. This is a common situation in high-low split.

A made low hand like

can improve to a high hand by catching a 3 to make a wheel, but a hand like

can never improve to a low hand. You're destined to play for the high half of the pot only, at the same time being at risk of having a low hand improve enough to beat you. As you're about to find out, this means that you can't play many of the high starting hands that you would play in a stud only game.

First Rule of Seven-Card Stud High-low Split

Play hands that will scoop the pot. This should be your objective in every hand you play. If you play a low draw, you should be trying to also make a straight or a flush. If you play a high hand, you can scoop the pot if no one qualifies for low. Low hands can win high and low but a high hand can only win high. That's because low hands can turn into straights and flushes. Be aware that if your first three cards are 9 and higher, you can never qualify for low in this hand.

THIRD STREET STRATEGY

Third street is the most crucial point in the game—and you've only got three cards! A decision to incorrectly call the bring-in bet is the most expensive mistake you can make. That's because a decision to call on third street invariably leads to calling on 4th and subsequent streets. It becomes a compound mistake because you'll be throwing good money after bad.

This section on third street strategy tips is the longest and most important of all the streets that follow. That's because you're really playing three different games at once and you have so many ways to make a mistake right here. Proper third street play is so important that you could probably be a winner if you played perfectly on third street and completely ignored the tips on how to play on 4th, 5th, 6th and seventh streets. A good decision on third street helps your hand play itself. The right decision on third street eliminates the possibility of making bad decisions on subsequent Streets. If you can learn to correctly call, raise or fold right here you will be a big winner in the long run.

Stealing the antes

Do you recall the very first third street razz tip? It's to steal the antes if you can. Only there are a couple of more things you have to know because you're not just playing razz here. You have to have a better hand to steal with because there's an increased likelihood that you'll be called. You can make the bad low hands fold but you can't always make the bad high hands fold. Also, you usually should not try to steal with three low cards unless you're sure it will work. That's because your steal attempt will build the pot and you may end up not qualifying for low. Raising and not winning is a bad strategy, if you think about it.

Steal the antes with

but not with

even though the first hand is a good high hand and the second hand is a good low hand. The difference is that you've already qualified to win high but you have a long way to go to qualify for low. If you try to steal the antes with a low hand and get called, you might not win any part of the pot.

> ### Second Rule of Seven-Card Stud High-low split
>
> *If you have an obvious one-way hand (high only or low only), then it must be exceptionally strong in that direction. If can't be just an average hand. Average hands get caught in the middle in high-low split games. You need to be compensated for the fact that you will sometimes not make your hand and you will sometimes lose with it when you do make it.*

Gaps in your straight draws are much more of a problem now than they would be if you were playing stud only or razz only.

is a much weaker hand in high-low split than in stud only. High pairs are also weak starting hands because of the very common situation of low hands starting with an ace making a pair of aces. A player holding in a stud game will usually fold. However, he will always call with this hand in high-low split and often catch another ace. This makes it unprofitable to play high pairs from the beginning when a player with an ace calls the initial bring-in bet.

High draws are vulnerable because low draws can turn into high hands. It's as if you're playing stud for high only and *everyone* plays!

Review your strategy in advance of the game

Decide ahead of time which hands you'll play and which hands you'll fold. Be specific. Have concrete reasons. Review this section. This will help you to consistently make the right choices for the entire duration of the game. Resist the temptation to loosen up as the game goes on. It is correct to make adjustments on the loose side if game conditions call for it but don't automatically play looser just because it's getting later. One good way to "play looser" without really playing looser is to raise the stakes later in the game but still play the same.

Also, ask yourself these questions:

1. What kind of hand do you have?
2. Does this hand play better heads-up or in a multi-way pot? For example, you have a pair of aces or a big drawing hand? The answers to these questions will help you decide how to play the hand.

Who else is going in my direction?

If it's obvious that you're the only one going high or low, then you *can* loosen up your starting hand requirements just a little bit. If it's obvious you won't be contested for your half of the pot, then the quality of your hand is not as important. It's still important, just not as important.

Play for low

You've probably heard this advice before. It's correct. Everything else being equal, low hands show more profit than high-only hands. You always know what it takes to win for low but you can never be sure what it will take to win high. You especially want to try to play for low when there's no qualifier because any hand can win low. If you're good at reading hands you'll be able to win just by knowing which way the other player is going.

If you start with a high-only hand...

Your chances of winning high go down with every low hand that enters the pot. That's because these low hands can turn into a high hand. Any one low hand probably won't beat your for high (as in regular seven-card stud) but when several hands start out low any one of them could make a high hand. And remember, they don't have to make a straight or a flush to beat you. Sometimes a low start will turn into two pair or trips.

An ace is a key card

Never leave home without it. Since an ace can be played for both high and low, it's like having an extra card in your hand. You're sure to be a big winner in the long run if you're playing eight-card stud while everyone else is playing seven-card stud.

If an ace raises...

Fold very often. Be willing to let an opponent win just the antes. Let him waste his good starting hand. About the only hands I would call with would be A-A-X or rolled up trips. It will be very difficult to determine which way your opponent is going until about fifth street or even sixth street and by then you will have invested a lot of money without really knowing what you're doing. Save your money for those times when you have an ace in your hand.

If a player showing

raises, how can you be sure what he has in the hole and which way he's going? A good player should be going high only but you can never be sure in a typical loose, low-limit game. You're going to have to fold very often.

Playing against an ace

This is what makes high pairs unprofitable in this game. Anyone who starts with an ace can easily spike another one to kill your pair of kings, queens or jacks. And, you have to consider the probability that a player already has a split pair of aces on third street.

The good starting hands are:
1. Three wheel cards
2. Three low straight cards
3. Three low flush cards (preferably with an ace)
4. Three low straight flush cards
5. Three-card 6 (6 and two lower unpaired cards)
6. Three-card 7 with few players. It's a weak low against a lot of players and probably won't make a straight.
7. Three-card 8 if it's suited *and* it appears your 8 is good for low
8. 6-7-8 if there's no raise. You have a straight draw with no gaps.
9. A-A-X. This hand plays best when you can get it heads-up.
10. 10-J-Q

There aren't that many good starting high hands in this game.

Starting hands that look good but aren't:
1. Three big suited cards

You're destined to play for high, your hand will be obvious and you will miss your draw more often than not. On the other hand, if you can get in cheap and you catch a great card on fourth street (about a 30 percent chance) you now have a playable hand. The thing that makes this a mediocre hand is the fact that you have to improve on fourth street or fold.

is an awesome starting hand in stud, but it's weak and vulnerable in High-Low split.

2. Three straight cards other than 10-J-Q

J-Q-K doesn't give you enough outs and A-K-Q means you have to hit perfect-perfect just to have a straight. All other straight cards are too low to play for high or they have gaps which means they are gutshot draws. Gutshot draws are bad enough in stud but they're even worse in high-low split.

is the only good straight draw in high-low split.

3. Big pairs

K-K, Q-Q, J-J, 10-10 just can't hold their own in a high-low split game. There are too many ways they can easily be beat.

4. A low hand without an ace, 2 or 3

5. A-2-3

Surprise! You'd think that the three lowest cards in the deck would be a good low starting hand but you'd be wrong. The problem is that with four cards to come, you need two low cards that don't pair you and if they do come, they may not be any good. What if you catch an 8? That will probably be your low if you get another low card but the problem is that someone else who started with a better high card (for low) will beat you.

is not nearly as good as it looks.

I'd much rather have

because you can improve it from both sides.

6. Any hand with two face cards

What are you trying to make with that?

An interesting situation regarding trips

In a quirky aspect of the game, certain trips can be a good swing hand. If you have trip aces, sevens or eights, you have a decent high hand and you could also possibly have a decent low hand. This is especially true if you're playing cards speak. Trips with a 9 or 10 low will often win both sides of the pot. Low trips can win high and low while high trips can win only high. (If you have three queens, you have a queen for low.) An added bonus to low trips is that you can be representing a low hand while no one will suspect you have trips for high.

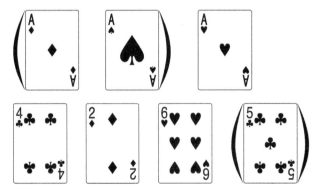

is three aces for high and a 6 for low.

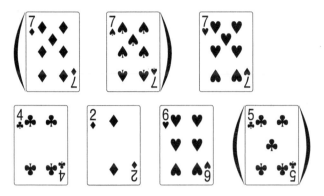

is trip sevens for high and a 7 for low.

If you start with a high hand...

You should usually prefer to play the hand heads-up. If you start with the highest hand, you will usually finish with the highest hand. But that's only when you can play it heads-up. Do whatever it takes to get it heads-up, including check-raising. Sometimes, you might want to wait until fourth street to make your move. You might even wait for fifth street when the bets double to check-raise to get the odd player out. An exception to raising and trying to thin the field would be when you're all going high and you have the eventual winner—for example, maybe you have a full house on fifth street. In that case, let opponents in so they can pay you off.

If you start with a high hand against several lows...

You always have to be careful when playing against several lows but bells, whistles and sirens should go off in your head if these low hands are raising each other. The odds are that one of three or more low hands will finish with a straight or better. The odds increase even more if those starting cards are good enough to raise with. It typically means that the low straight draws are open-ended and the needed cards are live.

If your third street card is a 10, jack, queen or king...

The other players will always know you're playing for high. And you will know the same thing about them. However, if you start with a low card, opponents can never be sure which way you intend to go.

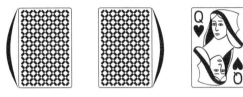

has to be a high hand, while

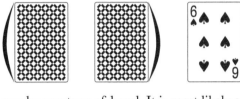

can be any type of hand. It is most likely a low hand but it could be

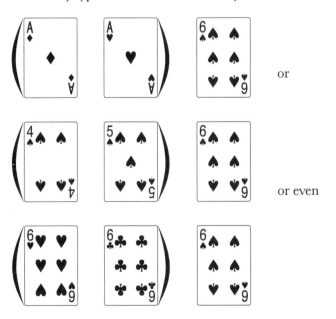

or

or even

When you start with a low pair...

All low pairs are not the same. 7-7-2 is a much better hand than 2-2-7 even though they're both the same low. That's because a pair of sevens can often win high in cards speak while a pair of deuces won't. If you and your opponent are both going low and you both pair a card, you'd rather pair the 7 than the 2. If you're going low and you pair one of your cards, it might as well be one of your higher cards so it can help you win high.

is a much better hand than

because even though both hands are a 7 low, a pair of sevens is more helpful than a pair of deuces.

When you have an average one-way hand...

Don't call raises, especially if it's a low hand that needs to qualify. The raise means that the other player is starting with a better hand than you and therefore figures to finish with a better hand.

Third Rule Of Seven-Card Stud High-low split

Don't chase in both directions. If you have a two-card high and a two-card low, you're really putting your faith in letting the cards you catch tell you which way to play. That's just plain stupid. Go high, go low or go both ways; but start with good cards, have a plan, and know what you're doing. Anytime you find yourself saying under your breath, "I'll let the next card decide whether I'm going high or low...", you're breaking every rule in the book. It's correct to occasionally vary your play but this is not how you do it.

What are you trying to do with that? It's like playing with only six cards while everyone else is playing with seven.

Fourth Rule Of Seven-Card Stud High-low split

Don't play any hand that has a 9 in it. And, of course, since it's a 'rule,' here are the exceptions:

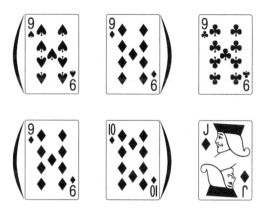

There aren't that many exceptions and if you do get dealt one of these hands, it's a decent start.

Straight draws

You can't make a straight without a 5 or a 10. When you play seven-card stud, some players looks for the tens because of that fact. It's correct to try for a wheel and small straight in high-low split, so, the fives are just as important. Having a pair of fives in your hand or otherwise knowing that two or three of them are dead, greatly reduces the chance that a low hand will make a wheel or any other straight.

Final bit of advice for third street

The advice you have just read is definitely on the conservative side. There's nothing wrong with that. It will keep you out of trouble while you're learning how to play the game. Following the above advice will help protect your bankroll, reduce the high and low swings in your bankroll, and make you a winner. However, every game is different, and has its own characteristics and unique factors—and they are always changing.

My final advice for third street is that you can relax some of your starting hand requirements and criteria for playing if your game conditions call for it. This is where experience and expert judgment come in to play. If your opponents are so bad that they are playing every hand and calling every bet, as is so often the case in home games, then it would be wrong for you to stick to a very conservative style of play. To win, all you have to do is play better than they do.

FOURTH STREET STRATEGY

If you have a two-way hand...

It doesn't have to be exceptionally strong in both directions. The reason is you have more outs and therefore a better chance of catching the cards you need to improve. There are more cards in the deck that will help a high and a low hand than just a high hand alone.

If you have a hand like

You have a lot of outs.

Ten clubs, any low card, and any high card improve this hand.

High and low heads-up

The high hand is always a favorite over the low hand unless the low hand also has a straight or a flush draw. A straight adds eight more outs to a low hand while a flush draw adds nine.

Always count outs

Count outs for everyone in the hand, yourself included. Look for needed cards on the board and use this information to help deduce other hands.

The Paint Rule

*If you started with an average three-card low and catch a **paint card** (jack, queen or king) on fourth street, **and** your opponent catches a good card—fold. Get out right there. You are no longer ahead, your opponent has four good cards while you only have three and the odds are that you can't catch up. This pot will be small—let it go even though you will probably not want to. This is fourth street, not "third street-with-a-bad-card." Fold.*

Remember this rule from stud?

Almost never slowplay

Fourth street is the time to:

1. Get the bad hands out.
2. Make the marginal hands fold.
3. Represent good hands.
4. Take advantage of your board.
5. Get it heads-up if possible.
6. Make the draws pay to beat you. If drawing hands take a fifth card, they will then take a sixth and seventh card and you may not win. Don't let that happen.

When everyone is going low...

The gaps in your cards become more important because you need to fill those gaps to make a straight so you can win high and low.

is a much stronger hand than

because the former hand can make a straight by catching one of eight aces or sixes, while the latter hand can only make a straight by catching one of four threes.

FIFTH STREET STRATEGY

Taking a fifth card

If it's obviously right for you to take a fifth card then that probably means you have a good hand and you're justified in taking a sixth and seventh card to improve your hand even further. However, don't go to seventh street because you're blindly following this advice. Do it because it's the right thing to do.

Can you scoop the pot?

Scooping should be your main goal. However, if you have a one-way hand it needs to be very strong in that direction to justify playing past fifth street. An obvious exception would be if you can see that you're the only one going in your direction.

Playing for low only

Fold if you don't have four low cards and no other outs. You need four low cards to go any further. If you have only three low cards with two cards to come, then you're just playing badly if you try to hit perfect-perfect on sixth and seventh streets.

Do you have the nuts or near-nuts?

Resist the temptation to raise even though it's clear that you're going to win the hand. This round is when the bets double and no one yet probably has a completed hand. You risk driving players out of the hand. Your board alone might scare them off. Wait for sixth street where everyone has the "I only need to see one more card" mentality and they'll call every bet.

You have a wheel or a 6-4-3-2-A

You can raise if you're the only one going low because the high hands will think they're not competing against you. You shouldn't raise if there's only one other low draw. The low draw might look at your board and correctly fold. You can raise against three or more low draws because one or two of them will certainly pay you off. It's not likely they will all fold. Make them pay for trying to make that 6 or 7 against you.

SIXTH STREET STRATEGY

Sixth street is just a continuation of fifth street. Almost no one will take a card on fifth street and then fold on sixth street. However,

If you made a bad call on fifth street ...

And you caught a bad card on sixth street —fold. If you made a good call on fifth street and caught a bad card on sixth street, call to see seventh street.

When you can't lose low

You have nothing to lose by raising. There is always a small chance that you could also win high and not know it at this point. In that case, it's good to have gotten in an extra bet with a winning hand. If you raise and split the pot, you haven't lost anything. You were going to split anyway.

SEVENTH STREET STRATEGY

Your goal is to scoop the pot; remember?

Failing that, as sometimes happens to the best of us, are you certain you can win one-half of the pot in one direction or the other? If you're playing cards speak and you're heads-up, you have a very good chance. If you're playing declare and you're reading the other hands correctly, you're in good shape.

Reading hands

What was your opponent's third street card? If it was a 10, jack, queen or a king, he most likely has a high hand.

A review from razz

A player going low must play at least two of his four board cards. This helps you read his hand.

To bet or not to bet

If you know you don't have the nuts in either direction, your best move is to check, even if you have a good hand in one direction or the other. It's not likely you'll be called by a worse hand if you bet. If you bet and do get called, it will be because you've got a loser.

If you're playing cards speak...

This takes the guesswork out of trying to read other hands when it's a close call on what to do. You will often win both high and low with hands that you would have never declared that way with. If you and your opponent both have weak hands, then it's very likely you will split the pot because a weak hand can't swing but it can be either better or worse than another weak hand.

If you're playing declare...

Declare your strength and hope someone declares with you. You will often win the whole pot because your opponent made a mistake of declaring the same way as you without being able to beat you. If you're weak, then try to declare the opposite of what you think the others will do. Everyone's board is very important. You will often be able to eliminate a player's choice just by looking at his board.

Heads-up with the nut-high hand versus an obvious low hand

You have the nut-high hand and he has the obvious low hand. Most players will just check because they know they're going to split the pot anyway. Well, I want to tell you that you should always raise anyway. That's because, in high-low split, the apparent low hand will often have hidden weakness and will sometimes really have a high hand. In this case, you don't just win an extra bet, you win the whole pot.

If you have

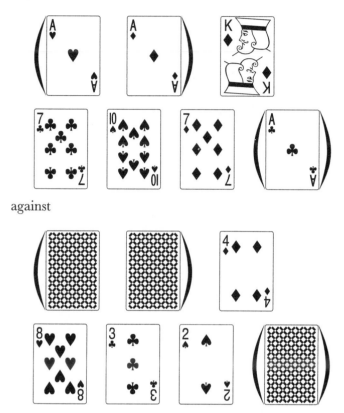

against

don't assume you're going to split the pot just because you know you're going to win high and he's obviously going low. That's because he could actually have

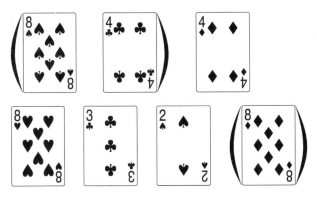

and also be going high. It's quite common for a good-looking low hand to actually turn out to be a high hand in disguise. Never assume. You have nothing to lose and everything to gain when you get in that extra bet with a winning hand.

If there's a bet after the declare in your game...

Well, then you're just in the best game there is for good players. Most poker experts agree that the one game that favors the good players the most and almost *guarantees* that they will never have a losing session (provided it lasts four hours or more) is seven-card stud high-low split with a declare and an extra bet on the end.

Lucky for you.

THE RULES, PROCEDURES & ETIQUETTE OF HOME POKER & HOW TO SETTLE DISPUTES & IRREGULARITIES

The purpose of this chapter is to help you solve the most common problems known to come up during a home poker game so you can get on with the real goal of a home game: Having fun with friends and family while playing a game of skill for profit. Every player has a responsibility to know the rules of the specific game they're playing, to be gracious winners and losers, and to accept unfavorable rulings with grace and dignity. However, the host of the poker game has a lot more to do. He has to be familiar with all of the relevant poker rules and procedures because he's the one who is going to make the rulings.

The host's responsibilities are to:

1. Read and understand the entire contents of this chapter. Most of the problems that will arise during a home game are covered here and it is so much easier if he can point to a written guideline such as this book rather than make up something off the top of his head.

2. Understand the big picture. That means that he has to understand and take into consideration all of the factors in the dispute and make the best overall decision for the game. There will usually be more than one way to solve the problem but you must keep in mind that different factors have more and less weight with each different specific situation.

3. Realize that it is not always possible to make a perfect decision every time. Do you best with what you have and beg everyone's forgiveness if you have to. Your decision-making will improve with time and experience.

4. Realize that the purpose of the decision-making process is to correct a mistake, to undo a wrong, and to make things as right as possible.

5. Understand the elements of a decision. They are: Tradition, Simplicity, Fairness and Efficiency. Tradition is important because it brings up the phrase, "But that's how we've always done it," and that's a very valid argument. In the absence of other factors, precedent is always binding. Simplicity refers to the nature of the difficulty of the problems. Is it a very simple, common, easy problem to fix or is it just the opposite. Whenever possible, try to reduce the problem down to its simplest wording or result. Make the question to be answered as simple as possible. Fairness is the concept of looking at the overall big picture and making a ruling that hurts as few players as possible without being overly beneficial to others. Efficiency means that you should solve the problem or issue as soon as possible after the issue arises. Usually, the best move is to stop the game right there and solve the problem before any more action takes place.

6. Whenever possible, rule in favor of promoting human relations, friendships and the spirit of the game above a strict reading of the rules.

7. Be willing to go against the written guidelines when it obvious that following them would result in an obviously unfair or wrong decision. It's not possible for a written list of rules to take into consideration every possible situation and interaction between human beings. That's why they're called "guidelines" and not laws.

8. Try to determine who, after all of the confusion is cleared up, is the true winner of the hand. If necessary, split the pot so as to invoke Rule #6, above. You also have the option of giving everyone in the hand their money back and starting the game over from the beginning.

9. Know that each different game has its own specific set of rules and what might be a correct ruling in one game would be incorrect in another.

10. Recognize the difference between a deliberate violation of the rules and an unintended transgression. Try to determine the player's intent when he broke the rules. Did the player intend to cheat or did it happen accidentally? Is the player new to the game of poker or is he experienced? A veteran player going through the muck during the play of a hand has a different meaning than when a new player does it. The seriousness of the infraction is a product of the offender's intent and experience.

11. Be familiar with common public poker room rules. They are:

   a. All games are table stakes. No short buy-ins, or one short buy-in, are permitted.

   b. Only one player per hand.

   c. You cannot play another player's chips.

   d. One bet and three raises are allowed, unless heads-up.

   e. Players must keep their cards in full view.

   f. No string bets allowed.

   g. Players are responsible for protecting their own hands.

   h. No eating or reading at the table.

i. Any player may ask to see any called hand at the end.

j. The decision of the host (floorperson) is final.

Regarding rule (j.) above: This is not strictly true. If you play in a public cardroom in most states, there will be a posted rule that states: "All disputes will be settled by the State Gaming Commission." This means that if you don't like the floorperson's decision and you can't get satisfaction by going up the chain of casino supervisors, you have the option of appealing to the Gaming Commission if the issue is that important to you. The poker room manager is required by state law to elevate your complaint to the Gaming Commission is you say so. You are the customer and the law was written to protect you. Of course, we are discussing home games, but if you play in a public cardroom, the above information is good to know.

What follows is a set of rules that are intended to be guidelines to help you settle common difficult situations in your home poker game. It would be good if everyone in the game were to read this list. There are many ways that this information could be organized and presented to you and I have chosen the *key word* method. A quick review of the key words now will help things go smoother later during the game.

ACTION

A verbal declaration of a player's intent, made in turn, is binding upon that player. In stud, picking up your upcards is a fold. Any gesture such as tapping the table, waving your hand or subtly moving a finger is a check.

ACTION OUT OF TURN

Every player has the right to act on his hand. The dealer should attempt to back up the action and let the play go forward as it should have the first time. Every attempt should be made to undo any harm by the out of turn action. A player who folded should be given his cards back if they can be positively identified. Notice that this rule goes against the rule that a mucked hand is a dead hand. It's the reason that the hand was mucked that makes this the better ruling.

ALL-IN

Players may go all-in for the amount of the bets they are able to cover. An all-in player may not be forced to fold. A player's all-in bet may not be raised unless it was at least one-half of the regular bet. A losing all-in player must rebuy before he can be dealt his next hand. That is, unless you're playing Poverty Poker as described in the "Home Games" chapter.

ANTE

There shouldn't be any problem with the antes because the dealer should be anteing for everyone.

BETS

A call made with a chip worth more than the bet is an automatic call unless the caller announces, "Raise." A player may not make his own change or splash the pot.

BOTTOM CARD

You should never deal the bottom card of the deck. Shuffle the burn cards and the muck if you need more cards. Do it before you deal the round on which you would run out of cards. This means that you will have to sometimes count the stub of the deck before you deal a last round.

BOXED CARD

A card that is accidentally turned face up in the deck is considered to be a blank piece of paper. Go ahead and deal the card to the player who was going to get it and then continue dealing to the rest of the players who are supposed to get a card that round. Then, go back to the player with the boxed card, deal him the next card off the top of the deck and use that boxed card as the new burn card.

BURN CARD

Whenever possible, the dealer should always burn a card before dealing a round of cards.

BUY-IN

A player must make a full buy-in to start the game. Short buy-ins after that are up to the house rules. A player who comes from a broken game does not have to have the full buy-in for that game. The minimum buy-ins are typically five times the big bet in both stud and community card-type games.

CALLING A RAISE

If a player calls a bet not knowing it has been raised, he may take his chips back and either call the raise, reraise or fold.

CARDS SPEAK

Cards speak is the concept that a poker hand is what it is regardless of any verbal attempt to call it, or to deliberately or accidentally miscall it. If you turn all of your cards face up at the end of the hand, it is the dealer's responsibility to help you read your hand correctly. There is one time, however, when it is acceptable to deliberately miscall your hand. That is when you have four of a kind. It has been a long-standing tradition in the poker world to allow a play to say he has two pair when he in fact does have four of a kind. Four of a kind is a very rare hand to have and this allows the holder of the hand to take a little bit more satisfaction in showing his pair of eights and his other pair of eights. Notice that this ruling recognizes the place of tradition over the usual rule of miscalling hands.

CHECK AND RAISE

Check-raise is an integral part of an overall poker strategy and should be allowed in any game. It is usually on the beginners who object.

CLOCK

A player has a right to take as long as it takes to figure out what to do when it's his turn to act, but there comes a time when enough is enough. If a player won't make a decision in a reasonable amount of time, then the traditional thing to do is to tell him that he has one minute to act on his hand. You then count down the one minute. If he still hasn't acted, you then count down ten more seconds starting at ten and ending with zero. If he still doesn't act by then he is considered to have checked if that option was available to him. If it was up to him to call, raise or fold, he has a dead hand. It's been my observation that only players who intended to fold from the very beginning will put you through this.

COLLUSION

Poker is not a team sport. The entire idea of the game is to match your wits against everyone else and let the money be how you keep score. It is unethical for anyone to advise a player on how to play his hand. And, just as English is the official language of all air traffic controllers worldwide, only English may be spoken at the poker table. I suppose this rule could be relaxed by a unanimous vote.

COMMUNITY CARDS

In seven-card stud, every player is entitled to a seventh street card, even if you have to turn one card face up in the middle of the table for everyone to use as a community card.

CUTTING THE DECK

A cut must consist of one card more than there are players in the game. Always have the player to the dealer's right cut the cards before the deal.

DEAD HAND

A player has a dead hand when he says fold or pass in turn, if he picks his cards up off the table, if he has the wrong number of cards for the current round, if his cards come into contact with another player's hand, or if he pushes or throws his hand face down toward the dealer or the pot in turn.

DEFECTIVE DECK

The hand is over as soon as a deck is discovered to be defective and all players are given back the money they put into the pot on that hand.

DROPPED DECK

If a dealer drops the deck for any reason and more cards need to be dealt to finish the hand, every effort will be made to determine what the correct stub of the deck is. The hand will then continue. If you cannot determine which cards are the stub of the deck, then you should reshuffle all of the cards known not to be burned or mucked cards.

EXPOSED CARD

Cards accidentally dealt face up when they shouldn't have been, or a card that flashes are considered to be exposed cards and are dead cards. It doesn't matter if anyone saw the flashed card or not—a flashed card is a dead card. This rule is designed to eliminate any disputes by players saying they may or may not have seen the flashed card. If it's possible for any one player to have seen it, then it's treated as everyone did see it. Cards purposefully exposed by a player are not exposed cards and he must keep them.

In seven-card stud, a player who accidentally has one of his first two down cards exposed uses that exposed card as his face-up third street card and his third card is dealt face down. If the dealer accidentally deals one player's seventh street card face-up, then he must deal all player's seventh street cards face-up.

In community card games, each of the blinds is entitled to have his first card not exposed. If it is, it's a misdeal and the dealer must reshuffle and redeal.

In high-only draw games, the player must go ahead and take the exposed card. In high-low games, the player must take the card if it's a wheel card. Otherwise, he gets a new card.

RANKS OF HANDS

The ranks of the poker hands is always determined by the standard order, however, home games that allow the use of jokers or wild cards make five of a kind possible. Five of a kind is the highest hand, ranking above a royal flush.

SLEEPER BET

This is a raise made by a player before he gets his cards or once he has his cards, made before it is his turn to act. It is usually allowed in most home games if the player announces he's making a sleeper bet before the action starts on that round.

SHORT BUY-IN

Only one short buy-in is allowed in most public and private games. However, in private games, a player may make any buy-in that a unanimous vote of all the players will allow him to make. A player may add on to his stack of chips, as long as he has chips and it's done between hands.

SHOWDOWN

The player who bet last should be the first to show his cards when the hand and the betting are over. If a player is awarded the pot and it is immediately determined that a mistake was made, every effort should be made to take the pot back and give it to the true winner of the hand.

SPECTATORS

Spectators are non-players and may not sit at the table or in any way disrupt or interfere with the game in progress. The host has the right to ask the spectator to sit behind a player or away from the table.

STRING BET

A **string bet** is made when a player calls a bet in one complete motion then tries to raise the pot by going back to his stack of chips after that. This is not allowed. A player who wants to raise must say or somehow indicate "raise" before he is finished calling the bet.

SUBSTANTIAL ACTION

Many times a decision will be made one way if there has been substantial action and another completely opposite way if there has not been substantial action. Substantial action has occurred if three or more players have checked or two or more players have bet and/or called.

TABLE STAKES

A player may play only with the money that he has on the table at the beginning of the hand. He may not add any more money chips to his stack if he runs out of money during the play of a hand. He must fold or go all-in. Money on the table that is hidden may not play. You may not take cash off the table or give some or all of your cash or chips to another player unless you are leaving the game. A player playing both cash and chips has the right to take his cash with him if he's going to eat or be away from the table for an extended period of time. All players are entitled to know how much cash and chips a player has on the table at any one time.

TIES

If two or more players have the same poker hand, then the pot, or their half of the pot, is split evenly between them. Suits are not used to determine winners of poker games, they are only used to determine who makes the first third street bet in seven-card stud. Reverse alphabetical order of the suits is used: Spades, hearts, diamonds and clubs is the proper order.

VERBAL DECLARATIONS

Verbal statements of your intent are binding upon you if made in turn. A verbal declaration made out of turn may or may not be binding, depending on your reason for declaring out of turn and whether or not the action caused anyone to fold.

WILD CARDS

The joker may be used only as an ace or any card needed to make a straight or a flush, or the best card needed to make a low hand. When using it in a flush, you may only use it as the highest card not already in the hand. You may not make double ace-high flushes and the like. That will only work when making two, three, four or five aces.

WRONG PLAYER GOT THE POT

That pot never belonged to that player and every effort should be made to take it back and award it to the true winner of the hand. If that cannot be done or if the next shuffle has begun, then the player gets to keep the pot. The reason for this seemingly unfair ruling is that the true winner of the hand had an obligation to protect his hand, read it correctly, assert his rights at the showdown and be aware of what's going on in the hand. Since he couldn't or wouldn't do that, he forfeits his claim to the pot.

HOME POKER GAMES

"The more wild cards and crazy rules, the greater the expert's advantage."

John R. Crawford

For the first one hundred years that poker was played in America, most games took place in bars, saloons, riverboats, gambling houses, or on the dusty trail. The enforcement of Prohibition in the 1920s closed public poker rooms. This led to the explosion of private games held in players' homes.

Home poker games are an American tradition. If you're going to host a game or play at someone's house, there are a few details that must be worked out in advance and there are some questions that have to be answered. You know why you're playing poker, and you know how to play poker. So, the remaining questions you'll have to answer are the who, what, when and where.

25 THINGS TO CONSIDER IN HOME GAMES

Here's a list of things to consider when having a home game:

1. Who's house are you going to play at?

2. Who are you going to invite to the game? Who are you *not* going to invite?

3. When does the game begin and end? Is it okay to leave early? Is it okay to play later than originally planned? How do you handle players who habitually show up late?

4. Who has the final word in deciding disputes or irregularities?

5. What food or drinks will be provided? How will they be paid for?

6. Will there be a rake or a time charge for playing?

7. Will alcohol be served?

8. Will there be a written set of rules? Can you all agree on the rules in advance?

9. Will you play with chips instead of cash?

10. Who will be the banker?

11. Will borrowing money during the game be allowed?

12. Can you agree on the ranks of hands? This is especially important if you're using wild cards. In that case, five-of-a-kind outranks all other hands.

13. What is the best low hand? Are you using the California Lowball scale where an A-2-3-4-5 wheel is the lowest hand? Or, are you using the Kansas City scale where the lowest hand is 2-3-4-5-7, with straights and flushes not being allowed in low hands?

14. What kind of cards are you using? Are the decks new and unmarked? Do you have plenty of replacement decks?

15. Are you playing table stakes or is playing on credit allowed? What is an acceptable maximum amount for an IOU?

16. Are the losers expected to pay up at the end of the game or at the beginning of the next game?

17. What constitutes a misdeal and what are the misdeal procedures?

18. Will there be a limit on the dealer's choice games?

19. Will asking to see what the next card would have been after the hand is over, otherwise known as **rabbit hunting**, be allowed? I don't think that it should be allowed because it's

pointless, slows up the game, and sometimes leads to arguments.

20. What happens when a player runs out of money in the middle of the hand? How are you going to handle the all-in question? Are you going to allow a player to draw light from the pot?

21. How many raises are allowed? Three, four or five? Some home games allow every active player a chance to raise, regardless of how many raises have occurred in front of him.

22. Will check-raising be allowed? I recommend that it is not allowed in low-limit games but it should be allowed in higher-limit games. That's because novice recreational home players have a preconceived notion that check-raising is a dirty trick. It is only as they gain more experience and skill, and perhaps read some poker books, that players come to see check-raising as a regular part of the game.

23. Will you allow straddles? Will you allow players to play the overs? Are you going to play with the kill rule in effect?

24. Can the dealer ante for everyone?

25. Who gets the odd chip when dividing the pot?

These are just some of the important questions that have to be answered to have a smooth home game.

TEN ADDITIONAL TIPS

1. Always cut the cards. Every dealer should offer the deck to the player on his right for a cut.

2. Some home players allow the deck to be cut again during the play of the game if the player who wants the cut donates $1 to the pot.

3. Do not criticize another player's actions or quality of play.

4. Be a good winner and a good loser. Nobody wins or loses all the time. Be friendly and don't hurt another player's feelings over his losses.

5. Do not needlessly delay when it is your turn to act. It is rude to deliberately waste everyone's time when you know what you're going to do anyway.

6. Keep all of your cards in plain view of everyone all the time. This helps reduce the number of misdeals and players acting out of turn.
7. Do not deliberately act out of turn.
8. Do not help another player with advice about what to do or not do in the middle of the hand. The rule is: One player per hand.
9. Do not allow spectators or kibitzers to hang around the poker table.
10. Do not take chips off the table during the game.

I think the best overall advice is to remember that it is a home game and not a public poker room or casino game. Everyone should conduct themselves in a relaxed, friendly manner with decisions and disputes settled in a way that keeps personal relationships intact. To do otherwise usually leads to the game breaking up and you don't want that to happen.

POPULAR HOME GAMES

ALPHABET CITY

This game is for the guys who want to make it really hard to play poker. The catch is that the ranks of the cards are by alphabetical order, rather than the actual rank of the card. Thus, aces are always high and the cards are ranked like this:

Aces

Eights

Fives

Fours

Jacks

Kings

Nines

Queens

Sevens

Sixes

Tens

Threes

Twos

A straight must be five cards in consecutive alphabetical order. Unless you're a member of MENSA, or really drunk, this is a tough game to play, but you can be a big winner at it if you're more practiced at it than everyone else.

The equivalent of an ace-high straight is A♣ 8♠ 5♦ 4♥ J♠.

ANACONDA

This is a high-low split game with many betting rounds and a lot of action.

Each player is dealt seven cards face down. There is a round of betting. The player chooses his best four cards to make either a high or a low hand. He then passes the other three cards to the player on his left, while receiving three cards from the player on his right. He selects his best five-card hand, while mucking the two extra cards. Then he arranges the order of the cards to roll face up one at a time. There is a round of betting. Each player turns up one card. There is a round of betting. The next three cards are then turned face up with a round of betting between each card.

When only one card remains face down, each player declares for high or low. Some games allow for an additional round of betting at this point, now that everyone knows who their competition is. The last card is revealed and the winners are determined.

Your best strategy for this game is to try to make a wheel, a 6-4 for low, or a full house of aces-full or better for high. Most other hands are losers.

You should remember which cards you passed because if you don't see one of them face up in your neighbor's hand, then you will always know what his hole card is. Conversely, make sure that you always expose one of the cards that you received.

Your best hint of which way the player to your right is going is in the first three cards he passes you. If he's going low, you'll get three high cards and vice versa.

AUDITION
This is a version of five-card stud where each player gets three down-cards and one upcard. Players must then discard two of their downcards so that they are left with one up and one downcard. All of the discards are kept safe until the last card is dealt face up. The dealer then shuffles the discarded downcards (so that no one will know who mucked which cards and therefore be able to get a read on a player's sole downcard) and reveals all of them. The lowest card revealed is now wild and then there is a final round of betting.

BASEBALL
This is probably the most popular variation of seven-card stud there is. The game is played as regular seven-card stud except that threes and nines are wild. The player must match the pot if he gets a 3 face up but nines are always free. A face up 4 allows the player to buy an extra card (for a predetermined amount). There are countless variations and the game is one heck of a lot more exciting than any written description of the rules can make it sound. Try it—you'll like it.

BLACK MARIAH
This is regular seven-card stud. The name of the game refers to the Q♠. If the Q♠ is dealt face up, the game is immediately over right there. The money stays in the pot, everyone who had an active hand must ante again and the game is dealt from the beginning again. Anyone who has the Q♠ face down splits the pot with the highest poker hand. If you're lucky, you will sometimes win both halves of the pot.

BLACQUE JACQUE SHELLACQUE
This is five-card draw where the highest poker hand splits the pot with the best blackjack hand. Since five cards in your hand will usually add up to more than 21, you will usually have a busted blackjack hand and

the highest poker hand will win the whole pot. Aces count 1 or 11, face cards count as 10 and the other cards count as their face value. Since there are only two betting rounds in this game, the game is best if you can play for the highest possible stakes, with the limit doubling after the draw. Players who regularly play $3/$6 limit Texas hold'em can comfortably play this game with a $10/$20 betting limit.

Any number of hands can equal 21—that's the easy part. But there are only a few hands that equal 21 and are also a good poker hand. Here they are:

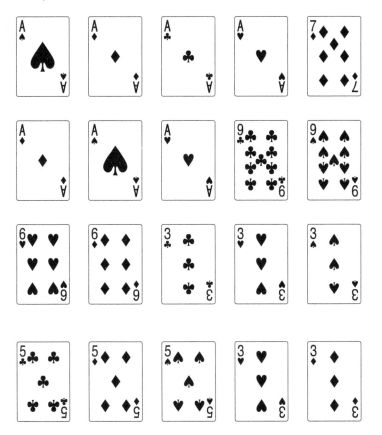

This game is surprisingly fun to play.

BLIND STUD

This can be any five- or seven-card stud game or any other stud game for that matter. All of your cards are dealt facedown. You can look at all of your cards but no one else can. You'll have to get your clues about the relative strength of your hand based on the betting, since there are no upcards in your opponents' hand to look at. The median winning seven-card stud hand is about three nines while the median five-card stud hand is about one pair of kings or aces. So, if it looks like you're going to end up with one of these hands or better, then you are a statistical favorite in the long run to be a winner.

BOB DOLE

That's the name of the game if you're fairly young. If you're a little older it's called Mo Udall. If you're older than that it's called Adlai Stevenson and if you're really ancient, it's known as William Jennings Bryant. These guys are all politicians who kept coming in second place in multiple primaries and elections. The second-best hand is the winner in this game.

Mo Udall was a U.S. Congressman who ran for the Democratic presidential nomination against Jimmy Carter in 1976. He came in in second-place in so many states that he actually made his campaign song "Second Hand Mo" (sung to the tune of "Second Hand Rose").

Adlai Stevenson was the Democratic nominee for president in 1952 and again in 1956. He lost in a landslide both times to Eisenhower.

William Jennings Bryant was the Democratic nominee for president in 1896, 1900 and again in 1908. He lost to William McKinley, Teddy Roosevelt and William Howard Taft.

Trivia: Bryant's Vice Presidential running mate in 1900 was Adlai Stevenson—the grandfather of the Adlai Stevenson of the 1950s.

THE BUG

The **bug** is the joker. You can use it as an ace or any card you need to complete a straight, a flush or a low hand. You can play any game with this but it's more fun if you save it for games that are traditionally played without wild cards. Instead of making deuces wild, which makes for four wild cards in the deck, the bug is only one card, and its use is limited at that. And it will sometimes not even be dealt in the play of the game. It's for conservative players who want a little bit of a wild card in the game, but not too much.

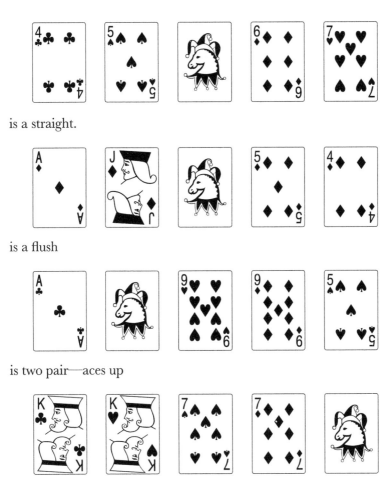

is a straight.

is a flush

is two pair—aces up

Joker is two pair—kings up

CANADIAN STUD

This is five-card stud with the last card dealt down and the addition of two new poker hands—a four-card straight and a four-card flush. A four-card straight beats a pair and a four-card flush beats a four-card straight. Two pair is the next highest hand.

The poker hands for this game are:

> High card
>
> One pair
>
> Four-straight
>
> Four-flush
>
> Two pair
>
> Three of a kind
>
> Straight
>
> Flush
>
> Full house
>
> Four of a kind
>
> Straight flush
>
> Royal flush

CENTIPEDE

This is seven-card stud where each player's position relative to the dealer determines what his wild cards will be. Twos are wild for the player to the immediate left of the dealer, threes are wild for the next player to his left, and so on. The wild cards do not change when someone folds.

The wild cards for each player in a seven-handed game (going clockwise from the dealer's left) would be:

DEALER	A	B	C	D	E	F
8	2	3	4	5	6	7

CHICAGO

This is one of the most popular variations of seven-card stud. The highest poker hand splits the pot with the player who has the highest ♠ in the hole. If one of your hole cards is the A♠, you are guaranteed to win half of the pot, regardless of your poker hand. If the A♠ is dealt face up then the K♠ is the boss card, and so on down the line. This game is also played as Low Chicago where the 2♠ is the boss card.

A player holding

is guaranteed to win half of the pot.

COUNCIL BLUFFS

This is Omaha high-low split with a qualifier for low. It's called Council Bluffs because you currently can't legally play Omaha in Omaha but you can in the neighboring city of Council Bluffs. The catch to this game is that the river card determines what the qualifier for low is. If it's an ace, 2, 3, or 4 then there is no low possible because you can't make a five-card hand for low with less than a five. If the river card is a 5 through king, then that's the requirement for low.

COURCHEVEL

This is Omaha where the flop is dealt before the first bet. You'll know 7/9ths of your hand before you have to make a bet.

CRYOGENIC FREEZE

This one's easy. It's seven-card stud with the first two cards dealt face down and all the rest of the cards, including the last card, dealt face up. The last card that a player receives, and other cards of the same rank in his hand, will be wild. A player has the option of not taking any more cards before the game is over, thereby keeping his last card wild. He's still in the game but can't have any more cards after he "freezes" his hand. Don't forget that a player who has only four cards can't have a straight, a flush or a full-house, but he could have four of a kind.

DOUBLE DOWN

Five-card stud where each player gets two downcards which are the downcards of two separate poker hands. He is then dealt two cards face up and he must assign each card to each of the facedowncards. Each player then gets two more cards and repeats the process, adding one card to each hand. There is a round of betting after every deal. You can't change the cards once you assign them to a hand. Highest hand wins.

DR. PEPPER

This is seven-card stud with the twos, fours and tens wild. That's twelve wild cards. The average winning hand is a high five-of-a-kind.

The wild cards are:

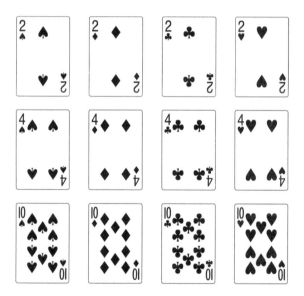

FOLLOW THE QUEEN

This is regular seven-card stud except that the card dealt face up immediately after a queen is dealt is considered to be a wild card. If you get the queen, then the next player on your left will get the wild card. If two queens are dealt in succession, then the next non-queen card dealt is a wild card. If a queen is the last card dealt face up in the game, then there are no wild cards. The wild cards can change during the course of the game.

FLUSH

The only poker hand in this game is the flush. Best five-card flush wins. If no one has a five-card flush then the best four-card flush wins. Then the best three-flush wins if no one has a four-flush. Most winning hands will be a four-flush so if you make one, be sure it's ace-high.

GUTS

This is two-card poker with an element of bluffing. There is an ante. Each player is dealt two cards and looks at them. He then holds them over the table while the dealer counts, "1-2-3-Drop!" Everyone who wants out of the hand drops their cards. The remaining players then compare their cards and the highest hand wins the pot. The players who stayed in but lost must match the pot and everyone must re-ante. If everyone drops, there is another ante and the game starts all over again. This continues until only one person does not drop and wins the pot. This is a pot-building game of nerves. The pots can get huge because they increase in size geometrically rather than arithmetically.

Sometimes, when the pots get really big, some players will hesitate to drop until they can quickly see who else may or may not drop. This is cheating. The best way to get around this is to have the player put a chip in a closed hand if they want to stay in. Each player then opens their hands at the same time. This game can also be played as one or three card guts.

The best way to win at this game is to have the biggest bankroll and never drop. The pot will eventually get so big that the other players will start dropping better and better hands and you will be the only player left. The stakes in this game can quickly get out of hand, so you might want to set a limit beforehand.

HEINZ 57

This is seven-card stud with fives and sevens wild. If you get a wild card face up, you must match the pot or fold. Facedown wild cards do not cost you anything.

HOUSE OF COMMONS

This is seven-card stud with the most common upcard being wild. If there is a tie, say three kings and three eights are face up, then the highest card—the kings are wild.

HURRICANE

This is two-card draw high-low split, played with either one or two draws. The highest hand is a pair of aces and the lowest hand is 3-2, unless you all agree that an ace is both high and low, in which case A-2 is the lowest hand.

IRISH

This is Omaha where each player is dealt four cards and must discard two of those cards after the flop. Obviously, in keeping with the rules of Omaha, both of the remaining hole cards must play.

JANE AUSTIN

In Jane Austin, the two and threes are wild. Since these are the lowest cards in the deck, they are usually not welcome in your hand. Now, you'll be glad to get them and this will help you use more of the cards you're dealt. The rules can be applied to any game, but work better if the game is for high hand only.

JOHNNY MNEMONIC

This is seven-card stud where the players must memorize their first two downcards because they're not allowed to look at them again. To win the pot, you must be able to correctly name both of your cards by rank and suit at the end of the hand but before you turn them face up. This holds even if everyone else has folded and you're the only player left in the game. If you miscall your cards, you don't win, the money stays in the pot, everyone antes again and a new game is dealt.

The thing that makes this game really fun (from the spectator's point of view) is that you're allowed to confuse and misdirect your opponents by calling out names of different cards and forcing them to forget what they memorized.

KANKAKEE

This is seven-card stud where each player is dealt two cards face down and the joker is dealt as a center community card. It's completely wild and belongs to everyone as their third card. The game then continues as regular seven-card stud.

LINCOLN

This is Omaha and all of its variations where the player is allowed to use only one of his hole cards, if he chooses.

LOW HOLE CARD WILD

This is seven-card stud where each player's lowest hole card and other cards of equal rank in his hand are wild. A common variation is to allow the player to take his last card face up if he pays a predetermined amount of money to the pot. Since a player would obviously believe that he's going to win the hand if he takes his last card face up, the cost should be at least the size of the pot, or nearly so. Another popular variation is to deal all of the cards face down and let the player decide which one he wishes to turn face up.

MEXICAN STUD

This is five-card stud where the first two cards are dealt face down one at a time and the players are allowed to turn either card face up as they choose. You then receive your 3rd, 4th, and 5th cards face down and you continue to turn up only the one card you choose. Your low card, and other cards of equal rank in your hand, are wild. Your low card does not have to be your hole card.

MULTIBALL

This is seven-card stud where a player who gets an ace or a king face up must immediately trade it in for two new cards. If one of those cards is an ace or king, he must trade that in for two new cards as well.

NIGHT OF THE LIVING DEAD

This is seven-card stud. If a player folds, he still gets upcards as if he were still in the game. If he gets a spade face up, he's back in the game for free.

PINOCHER

This is poker played with the 48-card pinochle deck. It has eight each of the aces through nines. Best hand is usually 5 of a kind or a straight flush.

POVERTY POKER

In this game, a player who loses all of his money is still dealt in as if he has the money to play. He gets all the cards the game calls for and he does not have to fold. When he finally holds the winning hand, he gets the entire pot (unless it's a split-pot game) as if he had contributed to that pot. This gives him real money to play with and it gives him a chance to come back in the game. You should probably have a rule against allowing a player to win more than one of these poverty poker hands.

QUICK SIX

This seven-card stud game is played only in a casino poker room that has a bad beat jackpot. Everyone is dealt the customary two down-cards and one upcard. The low card is forced to bring it in for a bet and everyone calls, usually for just $1. All players then check on 4th, 5th and sixth street, regardless of their poker hands. At this point, all players are still in the game, they all have six cards and they all have invested only $1 each. There is no betting until after all players have their last downcard. The reason for playing like this is to get the maximum number of cards into the hands of as many players as possible to give them the best possible chance of hitting the jackpot.

REMBRANDT

Usually played as seven-card stud but it can also be played as five-card draw. The face cards (paint) are wild. That's twelve wild cards, the same as in Dr. Pepper.

RUNNING MATE

This can be played with almost all poker games. The best (highest) and second-best hands split the pot.

SAN FRANCISCO

This can be played with most any poker game. Queens are wild and straights don't count. A straight flush is merely a regular flush.

SEQUENCE

This is a seven-card stud game. Once a 2 is dealt face up, all twos are wild. If, after that, a 3 is dealt face up, then threes are the new wild cards. And so on with fours, fives and the rest of the cards. You might want to play an otherwise unplayable hand if you're dealt a 3 or 4 at the start. Chances are you'll have a wild card before it's all over.

SEVEN AND TWENTY-SEVEN

This is a game where the hands are determined by the point values of the cards. The object of the game is to have your cards total as close as you can to either seven or twenty-seven. An ace counts as 1 or 11. The perfect swing hand is A A 5. That's because $1 + 1 + 5 = 7$ and $11 + 11 + 5 = 27$. Face cards count as one-half point.

Each player is dealt one downcard and one upcard. There is a round of betting. Each player then has the option of asking for another card to increase the point total of his hand. A player does not have to take a card if he does not want one. There is a round of betting after each player has had the option of taking a card or not. This continues until everyone passes. At this point the dealer then asks everyone again if he wants a card. If everyone passes a second time, the game is over. There is another round of betting and then everyone declares for high, low, or swing. There is a round of betting after declaring and then there is a showdown. High hand splits the pot with the low hand.

This game is also played as two and twenty-two, three and thirty-three and four and forty-four. The higher the number, the more betting rounds and the bigger the pots.

SPIT IN THE OCEAN

This is a five-card draw game. Sometime during the deal of everyone's first four cards, someone yells, "Spit!" This is the signal for the dealer to turn whatever card he currently has in his hand face up and that card is wild for everyone. If no one yells spit then the spit card is dealt after everyone gets their fourth card.

TAMMY WYNETTE

A seven-card stud game where your jacks and kings are wild if, and only if, you also have one or more queens. If you don't hold a queen, then your jacks and kings are dead cards.

TOMMY TUTONE

This is seven-card stud with the queens being wild. The player who has the poker hand that can dial the deepest into the telephone number 867-5309 (from the song of the same number) splits the pot with the highest poker hand. You cannot use a queen in the phone number and the tens can be used as 0s. You must do it in order so you need at least an 8 in your hand.

TWO DECK POKER

Actually, only one deck is used but you need two decks to make up that one deck. Ideally, you need one red deck and one black deck. Remove the clubs and spades from the black deck and combine them with the hearts and diamonds from the red deck. Shuffle well. From this point on, all the players in the game will know that every black deck card will be either a club or a spade and that every red deck card will be either a heart or a diamond. This game is for players who like to spend more time reading their opponents' hands and this setup certainly helps with that. This special deck works very well for all stud, draw and community card-type games. This game was created by poker writer Ken Warren.

WAVEFORM

This is seven-card stud dealt with the cards alternating up, down, up, down, up, down and up. Or you can start with down, up, etc. Start by dealing only two cards and then have a round of betting. This adds one more round of betting to the traditional game.

BLUFFING

Bluffing is betting with a hand that you know cannot win if your bet is called. Often, if you do attempt to bluff, you will be in the position of having a good flush or straight draw that didn't quite develop and you'll be trying to win the pot by making the other player fold what you believe is a better hand than yours.

Knowing when to attempt a bluff is often just a simple matter of knowing the pot odds on the river and having an idea of what your opponent's hand is. The mathematical rule of thumb for attempting a bluff is this: The pot odds must be greater than the odds of successfully pulling off the bluff. For example, if you estimate that you have a one in five chance of bluffing, then there must be more than five bets in the pot when you attempt the bluff.

Here's an example of how you would break even in the long run when bluffing. Assume there are five bets in the pot and you bet on the river as a bluff because you know you can't win any other way. If your opponent calls and beats you, then you are losing one bet in attempted bluff situations. If you do this four more times, and lose all four of those times, then you will be losing five bets in attempted bluff situations. If you try it a sixth time, and this time you win the pot, you get back those five bets, as well as the bet you made the sixth bluff with.

If there are ten bets in the pot, you can attempt to bluff ten times, and lose all ten of those times as long as you win the pot on the eleventh try, on average. It's the same thing as unsuccessfully bluffing twenty times and then winning the next two times you bluff. You will break even in the long run as long as the pot odds are the same as your chances of successfully bluffing.

The way to make a profit from bluffing is to have the pot odds be greater than your chances of winning the hand. In the first example, where you had a one in five chance of bluffing, what if there were ten bets in the pot instead of five? Then you would invest, and lose, five bets and then win ten bets when you won the hand. You would lose four out of five times but you'd be ahead five bets in bluffing situations overall. That's what pot odds will do for you.

On the other hand, what if there were only two bets in the pot when you attempted a bluff? You would invest five bets on losing bluffing attempts and then win only two of those bets back when your bluff succeeded. Clearly, you should not attempt a bluff when the pot is not offering you the right odds. That's because you are still losing even though you might win one particular hand.

Now that you know that the pot has to be offering you the right odds to attempt a bluff, that raises the question: How do you know what your odds of successfully bluffing are? And how do you know if you only have a 5 percent chance of bluffing and you therefore need twenty or more bets in the pot? Or how do you know that you have a 33 percent chance of bluffing and therefore you need only two or more bets in the pot? These are difficult question to answer precisely because it depends on your experience, your skill at reading your opponent's hands, your estimation of what all of the action up to that point means, and who the other players are.

You cannot bluff bad players because they are not astute enough to recognize the fact that you could be betting a good hand for value. They will often call, expecting to lose the hand anyway, just because they play too loose and it's worth the extra bet on the end to them just to see your hand. That's what makes them bad players.

It's hard to bluff good players because they recognize bluffing opportunities and they factor in the fact that you could be bluffing when deciding to call. And you cannot bluff a player who has a good hand, but you've misread him for a busted straight or flush draw. All of the conditions have to be right, and all of the planets must be in their correct orbits to pull off a bluff, especially when you're trying to run it through more than one opponent.

There's a little bit more math to bluffing that you need to understand and it has to do with how many potential callers you have when you attempt to bluff. To see this point, assume that it's equally likely (50-50) that each player will call when you attempt to bluff in the end. If you're first and there's just one other player, then the odds that you'll be successful are 50-50, or ½. That's odds of 1 to 1. If there are two players, then you have odds of one out of four (½ x ½). That's odds of 3 to 1. Three players (½ x ½ x ½) is one out of eight, which is 7 to 1. Four players is 15 to 1 against. Five players is 31 to 1 against. You can see how these odds increase geometrically rather than arithmetically. They get out of hand pretty quick. This is exactly why bluff attempts work best against only one or two players.

There's another factor that works against you when you're trying to bluff, especially when you're bluffing against more than two players. Some beginning and low-limit players feel that they are honor bound to call you with anything, especially if they are the last player in the hand who could keep you from winning the pot. The last player will often call your attempted bluff just because he's the last player, and not because he's considering pot odds or his poker hand. So, it pays to realize, in advance, who that last player is if you're thinking about bluffing.

Medium-sized pots are the most difficult to steal. There's a reason they got to be medium-sized. It's usually because an average number of players got average cards, made average strength poker hands and then created an average sized pot. If you try to bluff into one of these pots, you'll get called by—guess what—an average hand.

Very small pots are the easiest to steal because there are usually a very small number of players in the hand and they will fold slightly better than average hands when you bluff at the pot because they often correctly realize that they are not getting the right pot odds to call you.

Often, they will have only one small bet invested in the pot and they don't want to call a big bet on the river because there's so little to win by risking so much. If you're interested in bluffing at a small pot, it helps if you keep the pot small by not betting on the flop whenever you think it's safe to do so. You generally don't want to give free cards but, in those instances when it's correct to do so, one of the benefits is that it may help you successfully bluff on the river.

It can be very profitable to bluff large pots. The difference is, you may go a long time between winning bluffs, and when you do win one, the pot odds will more than compensate you for the times you lost. In summary, unless you have very good, specific reasons for bluffing at medium-sized pots, you should try to make most of your bluffing attempts at very small or very large pots.

FAVORABLE TIMES TO BLUFF

I've identified several instances in the game when you might be thinking about bluffing. You should occasionally review this list to help keep these points in mind.

1. When you have excellent pot odds
Seventh street is when you'll attempt most of your bluffing in stud. If you missed your draw on the last card, and the pot is huge, you should at least think about bluffing before checking and folding. Sometimes the pot is so big it's worth a try.

2. Against good players
An experienced player is capable of figuring out what you might be holding and giving you credit for it. He will then make a mathematical calculation and, if he doesn't have the right pot odds to call, he will fold. Bad players don't do this; they just call anyway.

3. In higher stakes games
These games have better players who are capable of folding one pair or two pair when they think they're beat.

4. When the flop didn't hit anyone

If you read everyone in the hand for starting with high cards and they then proceed to catch all low cards on fourth, fifth and sixth streets, you might be able to bluff at the pot on seventh street.

5. Against just one opponent

If I had to bluff at a pot, I know that I'd like to be facing only one opponent. It doesn't get any better than that. When only one call from one player can stop you from winning the pot, it's usually correct to go ahead and make that bet. Especially if the pot is big.

6. Faking a rush

If your seat is hot and you've just won five of the last seven hands, you can sometimes act very confident when betting in the hopes that your opponents will think you're still on the rush.

UNFAVORABLE TIMES TO BLUFF

Take another look at the above list of favorable times to bluff and then look at it from the other player's point of view. For everything you can figure out about the other players, they can also figure out about you. And you're outnumbered; there's only one of you to keep an eye on them but there might be as many as six of them to watch you. That's why it's so hard to get away with a bluff.

Here are a few more points to be aware of when thinking about a possible bluff.

1. If any player's door card is an ace

These players are hard to bluff because they will call you with just a pair of aces.

2. If there was a raise on third street

This indicates that there are some premium hands out there. You can't be sure that one of them is not hidden A♥ A♦ or K♣ K♠ and you'll get called when you bluff on the river.

YOUR OPPONENT MIGHT BE BLUFFING IF...

1. He started with two suited cards on third and fourth streets and another one did not come on fifth or sixth streets, or he's showing an obvious straight draw that did not get there

In a case like that, his only option might be to try a bluff.

2. It's just the two of you

If he's first to bet or if you're first and you check to him, he could be bluffing. He won't always be bluffing just because there's only the two of you, but it's something you should keep in mind.

3. It only cost him one bet to steal the pot

If your opponent can induce you to make a mistake that will cost you the pot, and it will only cost him one bet, you should be aware of that.

4. The pot is huge

I'd say that any pot with more than fifteen big bets qualifies in most players' minds as a huge pot and is worthy of a steal attempt.

5. The player betting on the river, and is therefore possibly bluffing, raised on third street and no aces, kings or queens are on the board

6. Everyone checked on any round of the hand

This usually means that no one had anything worth protecting.

7. Of course, whenever there are a combination of two or more of the above reasons to believe your opponent might be bluffing, it is more likely that he is bluffing

The way to make money on your bluffing attempts is to always have the pot offering you greater odds than the odds of successfully pulling off the bluff attempt. If the pot odds and the odds of successfully bluffing are the same, then you will not make any money in the long run. In those instances, I think it's best that you don't try to bluff.

MONEY MANAGEMENT

No style, type or form of money management will work if you play a game of skill without the skill.

Money management is a term that includes just about every aspect of poker playing. Everything that you think, say and do during a poker game is a result of trying to employ one or more principles of money management. Whether you're thinking about basic money management theory and principles, or just being practical, there's no escaping the fact that poker playing requires you to think about money management.

Mike Caro calls it "...the very silly subject of money management." And he's right. That's because no amount of expertise at managing money will make you a winner if you're not a winning poker player. At best, being aware of money management principles will help you hang on to your bankroll for a while longer, and you'll lose at a slower rate—but you will still be a loser. There's no such thing as someone saying to you, "Look, I know you're a losing poker player, but if you'll just follow these money management tips you'll be a big winner at poker.

So, it follows—to me, anyway—that the best money management tip might be: Learn to be a winner at poker.

Once you become so good at poker that you're a consistent winner, then you'll see that playing poker is like a job that pays by the hour, day or week. If you're a winner at poker, then all you have to do is divide the amount of your winnings by the period in question and there you have it—you know what your time is worth.

Since this is a book about seven-card stud and its variations, I'll keep this treatise on money management simple, if not short. Here's a list of thoughts, questions, tips and guidelines that will help you be a winner and increase your awareness of the very silly subject of money management.

1. Do not spend your poker-playing bankroll. Keep it separate from your other money.
2. Learn to perform honest self-evaluations of your skill.
3. Choose the game you go to carefully. Consider all of the relevant factors, the most important of which will be your expected profit per hour.
4. Don't be too impatient to play. This makes you play too loose and that's bad.
5. Pick a game that matches your personality. Consider the limit and pace of betting.
6. Protect your bankroll in advance if you're making an annual trip to Las Vegas. Break up your cash into the amount you want to risk every day.
7. Realize that poker is a relatively slow game compared to the other ways to gamble in a casino. It takes longer to get into the long run.
8. Pay attention to the rake. A large difference between poker rooms could affect where you'd prefer to play.
9. Don't forget about the one big advantage to being a poker player over the other gamblers in a casino. That is, you're playing against other people, and not against a machine that's programmed to slowly take your money.
10. Don't forget why you play poker. There are a lot of good, acceptable reasons, but earning money should be one of the top ones.

11. Don't forget that every World Series of Poker champion and every big tournament winner that you see on television once played at the level you now do. You have the potential to improve and get better.

12. Always play your best game. There's no need to deliberately make inferior plays. Trying to deceive your opponents by setting them up this way is vastly overrated and hardly ever profitable enough to make it a worthwhile strategy. Just always play your best.

13. It's okay to play in a higher limit game than what you're used to. Try to learn something.

14. You don't have to be the best player in your game to be a winner. Just be sure you make better decisions than the other players and the money will come.

15. Don't make big bets and raises when your statistical advantage is certain, but small. This will cause you to have big swings in your bankroll.

16. If you're losing more than 300 big bets in your usual game, it's almost certainly because you're a bad player compared to your opponents in the game and not because you've been the victim of bad luck. Many beginners will start by losing 300 big bets but if their more recent results show a winning trend, they will eventually start to win back their losses.

17. It's wrong to quit a poker game just because you're winning or losing. It's the reasons you're winning or losing that are important.

Once again, being an expert at money management won't make you a winner at poker. Only skill at poker can do that.

CONCLUSION

Thanks for reading this far. I know the phenomenal popularity of Texas hold'em has had a chilling effect on the desire of most poker players wanting to play seven-card stud. There used to be many seven-card stud tables in every Las Vegas poker room and now you can't even stir up a stud game in most of those rooms today.

But that doesn't mean no one plays stud, and that's why I wanted to write this book. The world is always changing and what was once the world's most popular public poker game is now one of the most popular home games.

I always thought that a book that didn't cover seven-card stud was an incomplete book. That's because stud is the core game and inspiration of dozens, if not hundreds, of variations of other poker games. As you can tell from the contents of this book, I think stud, razz, high-low split stud and all the home game variations are what a player needs to know to have a well-rounded stud education.

In today's home poker environment, it's not enough to be able to play only seven-card stud. You need to know all about those other games to be a well-rounded poker player, and after reading this book, now you are.

ODDS FOR 7-CARD STUD

ODDS FOR YOUR FIRST THREE CARDS

	%	ODDS AGAINST
Any pair	16.94	4.9 to 1
Pair of aces	1.30	75.7 to 1
Three to a straight flush	1.16	85.3 to 1
Three to another flush	4.02	23.9 to 1
Three to another straight	17.38	4.76 to 1
Three of a kind	.24	424 to 1
TOTAL	**39.74**	**1.52**

ODDS FOR IMPROVING THIRD STREET HANDS
If you hold A♠ A♣ A♥, odds your final hand will be:

	%	ODDS AGAINST
Four of a Kind	8.17	11.2 to 1
Full House	32.02	2.12 to 1
Flush	.70	142 to 1
Straight	.24	418 to 1

If you hold A♦ A♥ 9♠, odds your final hand will be

	%	ODDS AGAINST
Four of a Kind	.54	185 to 1
Full House	7.57	12.2 to 1
Flush	.70	143 to 1
Straight	.84	118 to 1
Three of a Kind	9.89	9.11 to 1
Two Pair	42.05	1.38 to 1

If you hold T♥ J♥ Q♥, odds your final hand will be

	%	ODDS AGAINST
Straight flush	1.49	66.2 to 1
Four of a Kind	.07	1431 to 1
Full House	1.50	65.9 to 1
Flush	16.56	5.04 to 1
Straight	14.91	5.71 to 1
Three of a Kind	3.19	30.3 to 1
Two Pair	17.33	4.77 to 1

ODDS FOR IMPROVING FOURTH STREET HANDS
Odds of improving one pair

	%	ODDS AGAINST
Two Pair	42.1	1.3 to 1
Trips	10.0	9 to 1
Full House	7.5	12.3 to 1
Four of a Kind	.5	199 to 1

Odds of improving Two Pair

	%	ODDS AGAINST
Full House	11.4	7.7 to 1
Four of a Kind	.5	199 to 1

Odds of improving Trips

	%	ODDS AGAINST
Full House	25.0	3 to 1
Four of a Kind	8.0	11 to 1

Odds of improving a 4-Straight

	%	ODDS AGAINST
Straight	45.0	1.22 to 1

Odds of improving a 4-Flush

	%	ODDS AGAINST
Flush	50.0	1 to 1

ODDS FOR IMPROVING FIFTH STREET HANDS
If you hold J♦ J♥ Q♥ K♥ T♣, odds your final hand will be

	%	ODDS AGAINST
Straight Flush	.19	540 to 1
Four of a Kind	.09	1080 to 1
Full House	2.50	39 to 1
Flush	3.98	24.1 to 1
Straight	30.99	2.23 to 1
Three of a Kind	5.18	18.3 to 1
Two Pair	29.05	2.44 to 1

If you hold A♦ A♠ K♠ 9♠ 2♣, odds you final hand will be

	%	ODDS AGAINST
Four of a Kind	.09	1080 to 1
Full House	2.50	39 to 1
Flush	4.16	23 to 1
Three of a Kind	6.66	14 to 1
Two Pair	36.63	1.73 to 1

ODDS FOR IMPROVING SIXTH STREET HANDS

If you hold two pair, odds your final hand will be

	%	ODDS AGAINST
Full House	13.04	6.67 to 1

If you hold three of a kind, odds your final hand will be

	%	ODDS AGAINST
Four of a Kind	2.17	45 to 1
Full House	19.57	4.11 to 1

If you hold two pair, odds your final hand will be

	%	ODDS AGAINST
Full House	8.51	10.75 to 1

If you hold a 4-straight, odds your final hand will be

	%	ODDS AGAINST
Straight	13.04	6.67 to 1

If you hold a 4-flush, odds your final hand will be

	%	ODDS AGAINST
Flush	17.39	4.75 to 1

If you hold one pair, odds your final hand will be

	%	ODDS AGAINST
Three-of-a-kind	2.17	45 to 1
Two Pair	26.09	2.83 to 1

ODDS FOR RAZZ

ODDS OF BEING DEALT SPECIFIC RAZZ HANDS IN YOUR FIRST THREE CARDS

First 3 cards	%	ODDS AGAINST
3♠ 2♥ A♦	.29	344 to 1
4 high or lower	1.16	85.3 to 1
5 high or lower	2.90	33.5 to 1
6 high or lower	5.79	16.3 to 1
7 high or lower	10.14	8.87 to 1
8 high or lower	16.22	5.17 to 1
9 high or lower	24.33	3.11 to 1
Two parts to 5 high or lower	13.76	6.27 to 1
Two parts to a 6 high or lower	20.63	3.85 to 1
Two parts to a 7 high or lower	28.89	2.46 to 1
Two parts to an 8 high or lower	38.52	1.6 to 1

ODDS YOUR FINAL HAND WILL BE....(FROM 3RD STREET)

If you start with 3♠ 2♥ A♦, your final hand will be

	%	ODDS AGAINST
A Wheel (5♣4♠3♠2♥A♦)	7.15	13 to 1
6 High	11.8	7.48 to 1
6 High or better	18.95	4.28 to 1
7 High	14.30	5.99 to 1
7 High or better	33.25	2.01 to 1
8 High	15.02	5.66 to 1
8 High or better	48.27	1.07 to 1

If you start with A♥ 2♣ Q♠, your final hand will be

	%	ODDS AGAINST
A Wheel	1.25	78.8 to 1
6 High	3.4	28.4 to 1
6 High or better	4.65	20.5 to 1
7 High	6.07	15.5 to 1
7 High or better	10.73	8.33 to 1
8 High	8.91	10.22 to 1
8 High or better	19.63	4.09 to 1

If you start with A♥ J♣ Q♠, your final hand will be

	%	ODDS AGAINST
A Wheel	.12	827 to 1
6 High	.48	206 to 1
6 High or better	.60	165 to 1
7 High	1.21	81.8 to 1
7 High or better	1.81	54.2 to 1
8 High	2.42	10.22 to 1
8 High or better 4.23	22.6	

If you hold A♦ 2♠ 3♣ 4♥, your final hand will be

	%	ODDS AGAINST
A Wheel	23.43	3.27 to 1
6 High	19.45	4.14 to 1
6 High or better	42.88	1.33 to 1
7 High	15.84	5.31 to 1
7 High or better	58.72	.7 to 1
8 High	12.60	6.93 to 1
8 High or better	71.32	.4 to 1

If you hold A♦ 2♠ 3♣ K♥, your final hand will be

	%	ODDS AGAINST
A Wheel	3.98	24.1 to 1
6 High	7.22	12.9 to 1
6 High or better	11.19	7.93 to 1
7 High	9.71	9.3 to 1
7 High or better	20.90	3.78 to 1
8 High	11.47	7.27 to 1
8 High or better	32.38	2.09 to 1

If you hold A♦ 2♠ Q♣ K♥, your final hand will be

	%	ODDS AGAINST
A Wheel	.37	269 to 1
6 High	1.11	89.1 to 1
6 High or better	1.48	66.6 to 1
7 High	2.22	44 to 1
7 High or better	3.70	26 to 1
8 High	3.70	26 to 1
8 High or better	7.40	12.5 to 1

If you hold A♦ 2♠ 3♣ 4♥ Q♠, your final hand will be

	%	ODDS AGAINST
A Wheel	16.47	5.07 to 1
6 High	14.99	5.67 to 1
6 High or better	31.45	2.18 to 1
7 High	13.51	6.4 to 1
7 High or better	34.96	1.22 to 1
8 High	12.03	7.32 to 1
8 High or better	56.98	.75 to 1

If you hold A♦ 2♠ 3♣ Q♣ K♥, your final hand will be

	%	ODDS AGAINST
A Wheel	1.48	6.66 to 1
6 High	2.96	32.8 to 1
6 High or better	4.44	21.5 to 1
7 High	4.44	21.5 to 1
7 High or better	8.88	10.3 to 1
8 High	5.92	15.9 to 1
8 High or better	14.80	5.76 to 1

If you hold A♦ 2♠ 3♣ 4♥ Q♣ K♠, your final hand will be

	%	ODDS AGAINST
A Wheel	8.70	10.5 to 1
6 High	8.70	10.5 to 1
6 High or better	17.39	4.75 to 1
7 High	8.70	10.5 to 1
7 High or better	26.09	2.83 to 1
8 High	8.70	10.5 to 1
8 High or better	34.78	1.88 to 1

GLOSSARY

Ace The highest card when playing poker for high; the lowest card when playing poker for low. Can be used simultaneously for both high and low in high-low split games.

Aces-up Two pair, where one of the pairs is aces.

Active Player A player who has a hand and is still in the game.

Add on In a tournament, the last additional chips that a player may buy, usually at the break.

Advertise To make a loose play or an apparently bad play for the purpose of getting loose callers on a future play.

All-in The act of putting all the remaining chips you have in the pot, usually before the hand is over. A player who is all-in can win only that part of the pot he was able to match if he has the best hand at the end.

B & M Stands for "bricks and mortar." Used to describe poker rooms that actually exist in buildings, as opposed to online poker rooms.

Baby An ace, 2, 3, 4 or 5 when playing for low or high-low split.

Backdoor Making a hand that you originally weren't drawing to or trying to make. For example, when you draw four consecutive hearts to go with the lone heart you started with to make a flush.

Bad Beat To lose with a great hand—usually aces full or better—to a player who made a longshot draw.

Bad Game A game that is unlikely to be profitable because of the superior quality of the competition or because of the very low stakes.

Banker Usually applies only to home games. The one player who is responsible for selling the poker chips, keeping the cash, possibly providing credit and keeping the accounting straight for that game.

Bankroll The money you have set aside to put into a poker game. This money is physically, or at least mentally, segregated from other money used for non-playing expenses.

Bicycle A 5-high straight: 5-4-3-2-A

Blank A card that appears to be of no help to you or your opponents. Also called a "brick."

Bluff To bet a hand that is likely to lose if called.

Bring-in The first, forced bet that the player with the lowest (or highest) card is required to make to start the action in the hand.

Broadway An ace-high straight: A-K-Q-J-10.

Bug A fifty-third card in the deck that can, by agreement, be used only as a fifth ace or as any card needed to complete a straight, a flush or a low hand. It is not completely wild like a joker.

Burn or Burn Card After the deal and before each betting round, the top card, which is mucked by the dealer. This is done to protect everyone in the event the top card is marked or somehow known to one player while the action is in progress.

Busted Hand A hand that failed to make the attempted straight or flush draw.

Buy-in The amount of money that it costs to enter into a ring game or a tournament.

Call To match another player's bet without raising.

Calling Station A player who calls way too much when folding or raising might be a better option.

Cards Speak The rule that your poker hand is determined by what your cards actually are, and not the strength a player announces. All casino games are played as cards speak.

Carvee A player who is being carved up in a high-low split game. For example, Player A has the nuts for high and Player B has the nuts for low. Player C has what he thinks is a good hand but he cannot beat either Player A or B. When Player C calls the maximum number of bets on each round and then does not win any of the pot, he will have been carved up by Players A and B, and is therefore the carvee.

Case Card The last card of a particular rank remaining in the deck.

Catch Perfect To get the specific card needed to make a hand, especially if it was a longshot draw.

Change Gears To change from loose to tight play, or from aggressive to passive, or vice versa.

Chasing Calling or trying to make poker hands that are longshots.

CARDOZA PUBLISHING ◆ KEN WARREN

Check To not make a bet when it is your turn, but remain active in the pot Checking is not allowed if a bet already has already been made in the round.

Check-raise To not bet initially on a round, and then to raise when the action returns to you.

Cold Call To call two or more bets at once as opposed to calling one bet then calling the other.

Come Hand A straight or a flush draw with one or more cards to come. A drawing hand.

Community Card Used when there are still seven or eight players in the hand on seventh street (or even earlier, if need be). Since there aren't enough cards to go around, the dealer turns one card, called a "community card," face up in the middle for all the remaining players to use.

Completed Hand A poker hand that requires all five cards to make the hand. That would be a straight, a flush, a full house, four of a kind and a straight flush.

Dark Bet To bet when it is your turn to bet, but before you look at your cards or the card coming to you on this round of betting.

Dead Hand A hand that is folded because it contains the wrong number of cards or because of some other irregularity.

Dealer's Choice A game where the dealer has the right to name the variation that will be played on his deal.

Declare To indicate whether you're vying for a high or a low hand, or both. This can be done either verbally or by holding a specified number of chips in your hand.

222   KEN WARREN TEACHES 7-CARD STUD

Door Card In stud games, the player's first upcard.

Double Belly Buster A straight draw where any one of eight cards will make your straight, yet your straight draw is not open-ended in the traditional sense. For example, you hold 8♣, T♠ J♦ Q♥ A♠. Any 9 or king will make you a straight.

Draw Light When you run out of money and instead of going all in, you play on credit. The amount of credit is indicated by how much is in front of you. For example, when everyone puts $2 in the pot, you take $2 out. At the end of the game, the amount in front of you is what you owe the pot.

Drawing Dead Trying to make a particular poker hand that, even if you make it, cannot possibly win.

Early Position The first third of players in a game waiting to act on their hands.

Eight-or-Better When playing for low, the stipulation that your fifth highest card must be an 8 or lower to qualify as a low poker hand.

Emergency Low A low hand that you weren't trying to make, that you may not realize you have and certainly would not bet on if you knew you did have it.

Expectation The average performance (profit or loss) of a particular bet or player over the long run.

Exposed Card A card that has been turned face up accidentally.

Family Pot A hand of poker where all or almost all of the players are still active in the pot.

Fifth Street The fifth card; the third upcard each player receives.

Fill To get the card you need to make your straight, flush or full house.

Flush A hand with five cards of the same suit that do not qualify as a straight flush or royal flush.

Flush Card A card of the suit that you need to make your flush or to pick up a flush draw.

Flush Draw To have four cards to a flush with one or more cards to come.

Fold To throw your hand in the discard pile, or the muck, and to forfeit all interest and claims in the pot for that hand. A verbal declaration of your intent to fold, made in turn, is binding.

Forced Bet The initial bring-in bet made by the player with the highest or lowest upcard, as determined by the rules.

Four-Flush Four cards of the same suit.

Four of a Kind A hand with four cards of matching rank, plus a fifth card.

Fourth Street The fourth card; the second upcard that everyone receives.

Free Card A card received on a betting round where there turned out to be no cost because everyone checked.

Freeroll Whenever you have a chance to win with no money at risk.

Full When discussing a full house, the three-of-a-kind is what the hand is full of. 8-8-8-5-5 is "eights full of fives."

Full House A hand with three cards of matching rank, plus two cards of another matching rank.

Gutshot An inside straight draw. For example, you hold A-K-J-10 and need a queen to complete the straight.

Heads-Up A game or hand against only one other opponent.

Hole The cards in your hand that are face down.

Implied Odds Money that is not yet in the pot but you believe will be in the pot by the showdown. It is an educated guess of what your pot odds will be when the hand is over.

Ignorant End The low end of a straight.

Joker A 53rd card in the deck that can, by agreement, be used as any other card in the deck. This makes five of a kind possible.

Kibitzer A vocal spectator; usually one who offers unwanted advice about how to play the game.

Kicker The highest card in your hand that does not help make a straight, flush, full house or pair.

Kill Game A game where the betting limits are increased—usually doubled—for the next hand only.

Late Position The last third of players in a game waiting to act on their hands.

Limp In To call another player's bet—as opposed to raising.

Live Cards Cards a player needs to improve his hand that are still available to be drawn as far as is known.

Lock An unbeatable hand.

Middle Position The middle third of players in a game waiting to act on their hands

Muck To fold and throw your hand in the discard pile; the discard pile itself.

Off-Broadway A king-high straight: K-Q-J-10-9.

Open-end Straight Four consecutive cards with room at either end for a fifth card to make a straight.

Outs The number of cards that will help your hand. For example, if you have two spades and you see two more face up on the board, then there are nine spades, or outs, that will make your flush.

Overcall A call made after there has already been a bet and a call.

Paint A face card (jack, queen or king).

Pot Odds The ratio of the amount of money in the pot compared to the amount of money that it costs to call a bet. For example, if the pot contains $42 and it costs you $3 to call, you are getting pot odds of 14 to 1. If it's $6 to call, you're getting pot odds of 7 to 1.

Rag A card that appears not to have helped anyone's poker hand.

Razz Another name for seven-card stud low.

Represent To play your hand in such a way that it is obvious to everyone what you have—except you don't have that hand.

Ring Game A poker game played for cash that is not a tournament.

River The seventh and last card in seven-card stud.

Rock A poker player who has a reputation for playing only premium starting hands and whose playing style is dull, boring and very low risk.

Rolled Up In stud, to start with three of a kind in your first three cards.

Royal Flush A hand with five cards of consecutive rank, from ace to 10, all of the same suit, for example: A-K-Q-J-10, all of hearts.

Rough Used to describe a made low hand that is not very good, given the highest card. A player who has 8-7-4-2-A would say, "I have a rough 8." Compare to **smooth**.

Rush Winning many pots close together in a short period of time.

Scoop To win both the high and low ends of the pot when playing a high-low split game.

Semi-Bluffing Betting with a hand that, if called, probably isn't the best hand at the moment, but has a chance to improve to the best hand with more cards to come.

Seventh Street In seven-card stud, the seventh, and last, card dealt.

Sheriff A player who frequently calls on the river so that opponents cannot get away with bluffing.

Side Pot A second pot in a poker hand that cannot be won by the player who ran out of money in the middle of the hand.

Sixth Street In stud, the sixth card; the fourth upcard each player receives.

Slowplay To play your hand in a much weaker manner than its strength would usually call for in order to disguise that strength for a future betting round.

Smooth Used to describe a made low hand that is very good, given the highest card. For example, an 8 for low is not a very good low hand; however, if it is 8-4-3-2-A, a player would say, "I have a smooth 8." Compare to **rough**.

Splashing the Pot Throwing your money or poker chips into the pot so that they mix with the chips already in there—which is disallowed in cardrooms.

Split Pair To have a pair when one of them is an upcard and the other is a downcard in your hand. In other words, you can see your pair but your opponents can't.

Split Pot A poker game where the pot is split between the highest and lowest poker hands or between two players with hands of equal strength.

Spread-Limit A betting structure that allows you to bet any amount between the preset lowest and highest amounts. The most common spread-limit game used for seven-card stud is $1 to $4 or $1 to $5.

Steal To raise on the first round of betting for the purpose of winning the antes (or blinds), regardless of the strength of your own poker hand.

Straight A hand with five ranks in sequence: A-2-3-4-5 through 10-J-Q-K-A.

Straight Draw To have four cards to a straight with one or more cards to come.

Structured Limit A betting structure that allows you to bet only the amount specified as the small bet and the big bet. It's usually a 1 to 2 ratio.

Suited Connectors Two consecutive cards of the same suit, like Q♣ J♣, 9♦ 8♦, or 6♠ 5♠.

Swing To declare for both high and low in a high-low split game.

Tell A clue from an opponent that helps you figure out what his poker hand is. That clue (or clues) can be made either voluntarily or involuntarily, and verbally or physically.

Three of a Kind A hand of three cards of a matching rank and two other cards whose ranks don't match: 8-8-8-5-2.

Two Pair A hand with two cards of a matching rank and two other cards of a different matching rank.

Under the Gun In first position; first to act.

Up Used to indicate two pair. A-A-9-9-5 would be called "aces-up."

Wheel See **bicycle**.

WSOP The **World Series of Poker.** The designated series of poker championships held every year in Las Vegas. The winner of each event is crowned the World Champion in that event until the following year.

World Series of Poker See **WSOP**.

GREAT CARDOZA POKER BOOKS
ADD THESE TO YOUR LIBRARY - ORDER NOW!

HOW TO WIN AT OMAHA HIGH-LOW POKER *by Mike Cappelletti.* Clearly written strategies and powerful advice shows the essential winning strategies for beating Omaha high-low poker! This money-making guide includes more than sixty hard-hitting sections on Omaha. Players learn the rules of play, best starting hands, strategies for the flop, turn, and river, how to read the board for both high and low, dangerous draws, and how to beat low-limit tournaments. Includes odds charts, glossary and low-limit tips. 304 pgs, $19.95.

OMAHA HIGH-LOW: How to Win at the Lower Limits *by Shane Smith.* New edition teaches low-limit players the essential winning strategies necesary for beating Omaha high-low. You'll learn the best starting hands, how to play the flop, turn, and river, how to read the board for both high and low, dangerous draws, and how to win low-limit tournaments. Smith shows the differences between Omaha high-low and hold'em strategies. Includes odds charts, glossary, low-limit tips, and strategic ideas. 176 pages, $12.95.

THE BIG BOOK OF POKER *by Ken Warren.* This easy-to-read and oversized guide teaches you everything you need to know to win money at home poker, in cardrooms, casinos, and on the tournament circuit. Readers will learn how to bet, raise, and checkraise, bluff, semi-bluff, and how to take advantage of position and pot odds. Great sections on hold'em (plus stud games, Omaha, draw games, and many more) and playing and winning poker on the internet. Packed with charts, diagrams, sidebars, and detailed, easy-to-read examples by best-selling poker expert Ken Warren, this wonderfully formatted book is one stop shopping for players ready to take on any form of poker for real money. Want to be a big player? Buy the Big Book of Poker! 320 oversized pages, $19.95.

WINNER'S GUIDE TO TEXAS HOLD' EM POKER *by Ken Warren.* You'll learn how to play every hand from every position with every type of flop. Learn the 14 categories of starting hands, the 10 most common hold'em tells, how to evaluate a game for profit, the value of deception, the art of bluffing, eight secrets to winning, starting hand categories, position, and more! Includes detailed analysis of the top 40 hands and the most complete chapter on hold'em odds in print. Over 400,000 copies sold! 224 pages, $14.95.

KEN WARREN TEACHES TEXAS HOLD 'EM *by Ken Warren.* This is a step-by-step comprehensive manual for making money at hold'em poker. 42 powerful chapters teach you one lesson at a time. Great practical advice and concepts with examples from actual games and how to apply them to your own play. Lessons include: Starting Cards, Playing Position, Raising, Check-raising, Tells, Game/Seat Selection, Dominated Hands, Odds, and much more. This book is already a huge fan favorite and best-seller! 416 pages, $26.95.

WINNER'S GUIDE TO OMAHA POKER *by Ken Warren.* Concise and easy-to-understand, Warren shows beginning and intermediate Omaha players how to win from the first time they play. You'll learn the rules, betting and blind structure, why you should play Omaha, the advantages of Omaha over Texas hold'em, glossary, reading the board, basic strategies, Omaha high, Omaha hi-low split 8/better, how to play draws and made hands, evaluation of starting hands, counting outs, computing pot odds, the unique characteristics of split-pot games, the best and worst Omaha hands, how to play before the flop, how to play on the flop, how to play on the turn and river, and much more. 224 pages, $19.95

CHAMPIONSHIP TOURNAMENT POKER *by Tom McEvoy.* Enthusiastically endorsed by more than five world champions, this is a *must* for every player's library. McEvoy lets you in on the secrets he has used to win millions of dollars in tournaments and the insights he has learned competing against the best players in the world. Packed solid with winning strategies for 11 games with extensive discussions of 7-card stud, limit hold'em, pot and no-limit hold'em, Omaha high-low, re-buy, half-half tournaments, satellites, and includes strategies for each stage of tournaments. 416 pages, $29.95.

GREAT CARDOZA POKER BOOKS
ADD THESE TO YOUR LIBRARY - ORDER NOW!

CRASH COURSE IN BEATING TEXAS HOLD'EM *by Avery Cardoza*. Perfect for beginning and somewhat experienced players who want to jump right in on the action and play cash games, local tournaments, online poker, and the big televised tournaments where millions of dollars can be made. Both limit and no-limit hold'em games are covered along with the essential strategies needed to play profitably on the preflop, flop, turn, and river. The good news is that you don't need to memorize hands or be burdened by math to be a winner—just play by the no-nonsense basic principles outlined here. 208 pages, $14.95

INTERNET HOLD'EM POKER *by Avery Cardoza*. Learn how to get started in the exciting world of online poker. The book concentrates on Internet no-limit hold'em, but also covers limit and pot-limit hold'em, five- and seven-card stud, and Omaha. You'll learn everything from how to play and bet safely online to playing multiple tables, using early action buttons, and finding easy opponents. Cardoza gives you the largest collection of online-specific strategies in print—more than 6,500 words dedicated to 25 unique strategies! You'll also learn how to get sign-up bonuses worth hundreds of dollars! 176 pages, $9.95

HOW TO PLAY WINNING POKER *by Avery Cardoza*. New and completely updated, this classic has sold more than 250,000 copies. Includes major new coverage on playing and winning tournaments, online poker, limit and no-limit hold'em, Omaha games, seven-card stud, and draw poker (including triple draw). Includes 21 essential winning concepts of poker, 15 concepts of bluffing, how to use psychology and body language to get an extra edge, plus information on playing online poker. 256 pages, $14.95.

POKER TALK: Learn How to Talk Poker Like a Pro *by Avery Cardoza*. This fascinating and fabulous collection of colorful poker words, phrases, and poker-speak features more than 2,000 definitions. No longer is it enough to know how to walk the walk in poker, you need to know how to talk the talk! Learn what it means to go all in on a rainbow flop with pocket rockets and get it cracked by cowboys, put a bad beat on a calling station, and go over the top of a producer fishing with a gutshot to win a big dime. You'll soon have those railbirds wondering what *you* are talking about. 304 pages, $9.95.

OMAHA HIGH-LOW: Play to Win with the Odds *by Bill Boston*. Selecting the right hands to play is the most important decision to make in Omaha. This is the *only* book that shows you the chances that every one of the 5,278 Omaha high-low hands has of winning the high end of the pot, the low end of it, and how often it is expected to scoop all the chips. You get all the vital tools needed to make critical preflop decisions based on the results of more than 500 million computerized hand simulations. You'll learn the 100 most profitable starting cards, trap hands to avoid, 49 worst hands, 30 ace-less hands you can play for profit, and the three bandit cards you must know to avoid losing hands. 248 pages, $19.95.

POKER TOURNAMENT TIPS FROM THE PROS *by Shane Smith*. Essential advice from poker theorists, authors, and tournament winners on the best strategies for winning the big prizes at low-limit rebuy tournaments. Learn the best strategies for each of the four stages of play—opening, middle, late and final—how to avoid 26 potential traps, advice on rebuys, aggressive play, clock-watching, inside moves, top 20 tips for winning tournaments, and more. Advice from McEvoy, Caro, Malmuth, Ciaffone, others. 160 pages, $14.95.

NO-LIMIT TEXAS HOLD 'EM: The New Player's Guide to Winning Poker's Biggest Game *by Brad Daugherty & Tom McEvoy*. For experienced limit players who want to play no-limit or rookies who has never played before, two world champions show readers how to evaluate the strength of a hand, determine the amount to bet, understand opponents' play, plus how to bluff and when to do it. Seventy-four game scenarios, unique betting charts for tournament play, and sections on essential principles and strategies show you how to get to the winners circle. Special section on beating online tournaments. 288 pages, $24.95.

GREAT CARDOZA POKER BOOKS
ADD THESE TO YOUR LIBRARY - ORDER NOW!

HOLD'EM WISDOM FOR ALL PLAYERS *By Daniel Negreanu.* Superstar poker player Daniel Negreanu provides 50 easy-to-read and right-to-the-point hold'em strategy nuggets that will immediately make you a better player at cash games and tournaments. His wit and wisdom makes for great reading; even better, it makes for killer winning advice. Conversational, straightforward, and educational, this book covers topics as diverse as the top 10 rookie mistakes to bullying bullies and exploiting your table image. 176 pages, $14.95.

MILLION DOLLAR HOLD'EM: Winning Big in Limit Cash Games *by Johnny Chan and Mark Karowe.* Learn how to win money consistently at limit hold'em, poker's most popular cash game, from one of poker's living legends. You'll get a rare opportunity to get into the mind of the man who has won ten World Series of Poker titles—tied for the most ever with Doyle Brunson—as Johnny picks out illustrative hands and shows how he thinks his way through the betting and the bluffing. No book so thoroughly details the thought process of how a hand is played, the alternative ways it could have been played, and the best way to win session after session. *Essential* reading for cash players. 400 pages, $29.95.

THE POKER TOURNAMENT FORMULA *by Arnold Snyder.* Start making money now in fast no-limit hold'em tournaments with these radical and never-before-published concepts and secrets for beating tournaments. You'll learn why cards don't matter as much as the dynamics of a tournament—your position, the size of your chip stack, who your opponents are, and above all, the structure. Poker tournaments offer one of the richest opportunities to come along in decades. Every so often, a book comes along that changes the way players attack a game and provides them with a big advantage over opponents. Gambling legend Arnold Snyder has written such a book. 368 pages, $19.95.

HOW TO BEAT SIT-AND-GO POKER TOURNAMENTS by Neil Timothy. There is a lot of dead money up for grabs in the lower limit sit-and-gos and Neil Timothy shows you how to go and get it. The author, a professional player, shows you how to reach the last six places of lower limit sit-and-go tournaments four out of five times and then how to get in the money 25-35 percent of the time using his powerful, proven strategies. This book can turn a losing sit-and-go player into a winner, and a winner into a bigger winner. Also effective for the early and middle stages of one-table satellites.176 pages, $14.95.

HOW TO BEAT INTERNET CASINOS AND POKER ROOMS *by Arnold Snyder.* Learn how to play and win money online against the Internet casinos. Snyder shows you how to choose safe sites to play. He goes over every step of the process, from choosing sites and opening an account to how to take your winnings home! Snyder covers the differences between "brick and mortar" and Internet gaming rooms and how to handle common situations and predicaments. A major chapter covers Internet poker and basic strategies to beat hold'em and other games online. 272 pages, $14.95..

I'M ALL IN: High Stakes, Big Business, and the Birth of the World Poker *Tour by Lyle Berman with Marvin Karlins.* Lyle Berman recounts how he revolutionized and revived the game of poker and transformed America's culture in the process. Get the inside story of the man who created the World Poker Tour, plus the exciting world of high-stakes gambling where a million dollars can be won or lost in a single game. Lyle reveals the 13 secrets of being a successful businessman, how poker players self-destruct, the 7 essential principles of winning at poker. Foreword by Donald Trump. Hardback, photos. 232 pages, $24.95.

7-CARD STUD: The Complete Course in Winning at Medium & Lower Limits *by Roy West.* Learn the latest strategies for winning at $1-$4 spread-limit up to $10/$20 fixed-limit games. Covers starting hands, 3rd-7th street strategy, overcards, selective aggressiveness, reading hands, pro secrets, psychology, and more in an informal 42 lesson format. Includes bonus chapter on 7-stud tournament strategy by Tom McEvoy. 224 pages, $19.95.

DOYLE BRUNSON'S EXCITING BOOKS
ADD THESE TO YOUR COLLECTION - ORDER NOW!

SUPER SYSTEM *by Doyle Brunson*. This classic book is considered by the pros to be the best book ever written on poker! Jam-packed with advanced strategies, theories, tactics and money-making techniques, no serious poker player can afford to be without this hard-hitting information. Includes fifty pages of the most precise poker statistics ever published. Features chapters written by poker's biggest superstars, such as Dave Sklansky, Mike Caro, Chip Reese, Joey Hawthorne, Bobby Baldwin, and Doyle. Essential strategies, advanced play, and no-nonsense winning advice on making money at 7-card stud (razz, high-low split, cards speak, and declare), draw poker, lowball, and hold'em (limit and no-limit). This is a must-read for any serious poker player. 628 pages, $29.95.

SUPER SYSTEM 2 *by Doyle Brunson*. The most anticipated poker book ever, SS2 expands upon the original with more games and professional secrets from the best in the world. Superstar contributors include Daniel Negreanu, winner of multiple WSOP gold bracelets and 2004 Poker Player of the Year; Lyle Berman, 3-time WSOP gold bracelet winner, founder of the World Poker Tour, and super-high stakes cash player; Bobby Baldwin, 1978 World Champion; Johnny Chan, 2-time World Champion and 10-time WSOP bracelet winner; Mike Caro, poker's greatest researcher, theorist, and instructor; Jennifer Harman, the world's top female player and one of ten best overall; Todd Brunson, winner of more than 20 tournaments; and Crandell Addington, no-limit hold'em legend. 672 pgs, $34.95.

CARO'S GUIDE TO DOYLE BRUNSON'S SUPER SYSTEM *by Mike Caro*. Working with World Champion Doyle Brunson, the legendary Mike Caro has created a fresh look to the "Bible" of all poker books, adding new and personal insights that help you understand the original work. Caro breaks 36 concepts into either "Analysis, Commentary, Concept, Mission, Play-By-Play, Psychology, Statistics, Story, or Strategy. Lots of illustrations and winning concepts give even more value to this great work. 86 pages, 8 1/2 x 11, $19.95.

ACCORDING TO DOYLE *by Doyle Brunson*. Learn what it takes to be a great poker player by climbing inside the mind of poker's most famous champion. Fascinating anecdotes and adventures from Doyle's early career playing poker in roadhouses are interspersed with lessons from the champion who has made more money at poker than anyone else in history. Learn what makes a great player tick, how he approaches the game, and receive candid, powerful advice from the legend himself. 208 pages, $14.95.

MY 50 MOST MEMORABLE HANDS *by Doyle Brunson*. This instant classic relives the most incredible hands by the greatest poker player of all time. Great players, legends, and poker's most momentous events march in and out of fifty years of unforgettable hands. Sit side-by-side with Doyle as he replays the excitement and life-changing moments of the most thrilling and crucial hands in the history of poker: from his early games as a rounder in the rough-and-tumble "Wild West" years—where a man was more likely to get shot as he was to get a straight flush—to the nail-biting excitement of his two world championship titles. Relive million dollar hands and the high stakes tension of sidestepping police, hijackers and murderers. A thrilling collection of stories and sage poker advice. 168 pages, $14.95.

ONLINE POKER *by Doyle Brunson*. Ten compelling chapters show you how to get started, explain the safety features which lets you play worry-free, and lets you in on the strategies that Doyle himself uses to beat players in cyberspace. Poker is poker, as Doyle explains, but there are also strategies that only apply to the online version, where the players are weaker!—and Doyle reveals them all in this book. 192 pages, illustrations, $14.95.

BOBBY BALDWIN'S WINNING POKER SECRETS *by Mike Caro with Bobby Baldwin*. The fascinating account of 1978 World Champion Bobby Baldwin's early career playing poker against other legends is packed with valuable insights. Covers the common mistakes average players make at seven poker variations and the dynamic winning concepts needed for success. Endorsed by superstars Doyle Brunson and Amarillo Slim. 208 pages, $14.95.

MIKE CARO'S EXCITING WORK
POWERFUL BOOKS YOU **MUST** HAVE

CARO'S MOST PROFITABLE HOLD'EM ADVICE *by Mike Caro*. When Mike Caro writes a book on winning, all poker players take notice. And they should: The "Mad Genius of Poker" has influenced just about every professional player and world champion alive. You'll journey far beyond the traditional tactical tools offered in most poker books and for the first time, have access to the entire missing arsenal of strategies left out of everything you've ever seen or experienced. Caro's first major work in two decades is packed with hundreds of powerful ideas, concepts, and strategies, many of which will be new to you—they have never been made available to the general public. This book represents Caro's lifelong research into beating the game of hold em. 408 pages, $24.95

MASTERING HOLD'EM AND OMAHA *by Mike Caro and Mike Cappelletti*. Learn the professional secrets to mastering the two most popular games of big-money poker: hold'em and Omaha. This is a thinking player's book, packed with ideas, with the focus is on making you a winning player. You'll learn everything from the strategies for play on the preflop, flop, turn and river, to image control and taking advantage of players stuck in losing patterns. You'll also learn how to create consistent winning patterns, use perception to gain an edge, avoid common errors, go after and win default pots, recognize and use the various types of raises, play marginal hands for profit, the importance of being loved or feared, and Cappelletti's unique point count system for Omaha. 328 pages, $19.95.

CARO'S BOOK OF POKER TELLS *by Mike Caro*. One of the ten greatest books written on poker, this must-have book should be in every player's library. If you're serious about winning, you'll realize that most of the profit comes from being able to read your opponents. Caro reveals the the secrets of interpreting *tells*—physical reactions that reveal information about a player's cards—such as shrugs, sighs, shaky hands, eye contact, and many more. Learn when opponents are bluffing, when they aren't and why—based solely on their mannerisms. Over 170 photos of players in action and play-by-play examples show the actual tells. These powerful ideas will give you the decisive edge. 320 pages, $24.95.

CARO'S FUNDAMENTAL SECRETS OF WINNING POKER *by Mike Caro*. Learn the essential strategies, concepts, and plays that comprise the very foundation of winning poker play. Learn to win more from weak players, equalize stronger players, bluff a bluffer, win big pots, where to sit against weak players, and the six factors of strategic table image. Includes selected tips on hold 'em, 7 stud, draw, lowball, tournaments, more. 160 pages, $12.95.

CARO'S PROFESSIONAL POKER REPORTS

Each of these three powerful insider poker reports is centered around a daily mission, with the goal of adding one weapon per day to your arsenal. Theoretical concepts and practical situations are mixed together for fast in-depth learning. For serious players.

11 DAYS TO 7-STUD SUCCESS. Bluffing, playing and defending pairs, different strategies for the different streets, analyzing situations—lots of information within. One advantage is gained each day. A quick and powerful method to 7-stud winnings. Essential. Signed, numbered. $19.95.

12 DAYS TO HOLD'EM SUCCESS. Positional thinking, playing and defending against mistakes, small pairs, flop situations, playing the river, are just some sample lessons. Guaranteed to make you a better player. Very popular. Signed, numbered. $19.95.

PROFESSIONAL 7-STUD REPORT. When to call, pass, and raise, playing starting hands, aggressive play, 4th and 5th street concepts, lots more. Tells how to read an opponent's starting hand, plus sophisticated advanced strategies. Important revision for serious players. Signed, numbered. $19.95.

THE CHAMPIONSHIP SERIES
POWERFUL INFORMATION YOU <u>MUST</u> HAVE

CHAMPIONSHIP NO-LIMIT & POT-LIMIT HOLD'EM *by T. J. Cloutier & Tom McEvoy.* The bible for winning pot-limit and no-limit hold'em tournaments gives you all the answers to your most important questions: How do you get inside your opponents' heads and learn how to beat them at their own game? How can you tell how much to bet, raise, and reraise in no-limit hold'em? When can you bluff? How do you set up your opponents in pot-limit hold'em so that you can win a monster pot? What are the best strategies for winning no-limit and pot-limit tournaments, satellites, and supersatellites? Rock-solid and inspired advice you can bank on from two of the most recognizable figures in poker. 304 pages, $29.95.

CHAMPIONSHIP HOLD'EM *by T. J. Cloutier & Tom McEvoy.* Hard-hitting hold'em the way it's played *today* in both limit cash games and tournaments. Get killer advice on how to win more money in rammin'-jammin' games, kill-pot, jackpot, shorthanded, and full table cash games. You'll learn the thinking process for preflop, flop, turn, and river play with specific suggestions for what to do when good or bad things happen. Includes play-by-play analyses, advice on how to maximize profits against rocks in tight games, weaklings in loose games, experts in solid games, plus tournament strategies for small buy-in, big buy-in, rebuy, add-on, satellite and big-field major tournaments. Wow! 392 pages, $29.95.

CHAMPIONSHIP OMAHA (Omaha High-Low, Pot-limit Omaha, Limit High Omaha) *by Tom McEvoy & T.J. Cloutier.* Clearly-written strategies and powerful advice from Cloutier and McEvoy who have won four World Series of Poker Omaha titles. You'll learn how to beat low-limit and high-stakes games, play against loose and tight opponents, and the differing strategies for rebuy and freezeout tournaments. Learn the best starting hands, when slowplaying a big hand is dangerous, what danglers are (and why winners don't play them), why you sometimes fold the nuts on the flop and would be correct in doing so, and overall, how you can win a lot of money at Omaha! 296 pages, illustrations, $29.95.

CHAMPIONSHIP HOLD'EM TOURNAMENT HANDS *by T. J. Cloutier & Tom McEvoy.* An absolute must for hold'em tournament players, two legends show you how to become a winning tournament player at both limit and no-limit hold'em games. Get inside the authors' heads as they think their way through the correct strategy at 57 limit and no-limit starting hands. Cloutier & McEvoy show you how to use skill and intuition to play strategic hands for maximum profit in real tournament scenarios and how 45 key hands were played by champions in turnaround situations at the WSOP. Gain tremendous insights into how tournament poker is played at the highest levels. 368 pages, $29.95.

CHAMPIONSHIP HOLD'EM SATELLITE STRATEGY *by Brad Dougherty & Tom McEvoy.* Every year satellite players win their way into the $10,000 WSOP buy-in and emerge as millionaires or champions. You can too! Learn the specific, proven strategies for winning almost any satellite from two world champions. Covers the ten ways to win a seat at the WSOP, how to win limit hold'em and no-limit hold'em satellites, one-table satellites, online satellites, and the final table of super satellites. Includes a special chapter on no-limit hold'em satellites! 320 pages, $29.95.

HOW TO WIN THE CHAMPIONSHIP: Hold'em Strategies for the Final Table, *by T.J. Cloutier.* If you're hungry to win a championship, this is the book that will pave the way! T.J. Cloutier, the greatest tournament poker player ever—he has won 60 major tournament titles and appeared at 39 final tables at the WSOP, both more than any other player in the history of poker—shows how to get to the final table where the big money is made and then how to win it all. You'll learn how to build up enough chips to make it through the early and middle rounds and then how to employ T.J.'s own strategies to outmaneuver opponents at the final table and win championships. You'll learn how to adjust your play depending upon stack sizes, antes/blinds, table position, opponents styles, chip counts, and the specific strategies for six-handed, three handed, and heads-up play. 288 pages, $29.95.

POWERFUL WINNING POKER SIMULATIONS
A MUST FOR SERIOUS PLAYERS WITH A COMPUTER!
IBM compatible CD ROM Win 95, 98, 2000, NT, ME, XP

These incredible full color poker simulations are the best method to improve your game. Computer opponents play like real players. All games let you set the limits and rake and have fully programmable players, plus stat tracking, and Hand Analyzer for starting hands. MIke Caro, the world's foremost poker theoretician says, "Amazing... a steal for under $500... get it, it's great." Includes free phone support. "Smart Advisor" gives expert advice for every play!

1. TURBO TEXAS HOLD'EM FOR WINDOWS - $59.95. Choose which players, and how many (2-10) you want to play, create loose/tight games, and control check-raising, bluffing, position, sensitivity to pot odds, and more! Also, instant replay, pop-up odds, Professional Advisor keeps track of play statistics. Free bonus: Hold'em Hand Analyzer analyzes all 169 pocket hands in detail and their win rates under any conditions you set. Caro says this "hold'em software is the most powerful ever created." Great product!

2. TURBO SEVEN-CARD STUD FOR WINDOWS - $59.95. Create any conditions of play; choose number of players (2-8), bet amounts, fixed or spread limit, bring-in method, tight/loose conditions, position, reaction to board, number of dead cards, and stack deck to create special conditions. Features instant replay. Terrific stat reporting includes analysis of starting cards, 3-D bar charts, and graphs. Play interactively and run high speed simulation to test strategies. Hand Analyzer analyzes starting hands in detail. Wow!

3. TURBO OMAHA HIGH-LOW SPLIT FOR WINDOWS - $59.95. Specify any playing conditions; betting limits, number of raises, blind structures, button position, aggressiveness/ passiveness of opponents, number of players (2-10), types of hands dealt, blinds, position, board reaction, and specify flop, turn, and river cards! Choose opponents and use provided point count or create your own. Statistical reporting, instant replay, pop-up odds high speed simulation to test strategies, amazing Hand Analyzer, and much more!

4. TURBO OMAHA HIGH FOR WINDOWS - $59.95. Same features as above, but tailored for Omaha High only. Caro says program is "an electrifying research tool...it can clearly be worth thousands of dollars to any serious player. A must for Omaha High players.

5. TURBO 7 STUD 8 OR BETTER - $59.95. Brand new with all the features you expect from the Wilson Turbo products: the latest artificial intelligence, instant advice and exact odds, play versus 2-7 opponents, enhanced data charts that can be exported or printed, the ability to fold out of turn and immediately go to the next hand, ability to peek at opponents hand, optional warning mode that warns you if a play disagrees with the advisor, and automatic mode that runs up to 50 tests unattended. Tough computer players vary their styles for a great game.

---

6. TOURNAMENT TEXAS HOLD'EM - $39.95

Set-up for tournament practice and play, this realistic simulation pits you against celebrity look-alikes. Tons of options let you control tournament size with 10 to 300 entrants, select limits, ante, rake, blind structures, freezeouts, number of rebuys and competition level of opponents. Pop-up status report shows how you're doing vs. the competition. Save tournaments in progress to play again later. Additional feature allows quick folds on finished hands.

FREE!
Poker & Gaming Magazines

www.cardozapub.com

3 GREAT REASONS TO VISIT NOW!

1. FREE GAMING MAGAZINES
Go online now and read all about the exciting world of poker, gambling, and online gaming. Our magazines are packed with tips, expert strategies, tournament schedules and results, gossip, news, contests, polls, exclusive discounts on hotels, travel, and more to our readers, prepublication book discounts, free-money bonuses for online sites, and words of wisdom from the world's top experts and authorities. Also, you can sign up for Avery Cardoza's free email newsletters.

2. MORE THAN 200 BOOKS TO MAKE YOU A WINNER
We are the world's largest publisher of gaming and gambling books and represent a who's who of the greatest players and writers on poker, gambling, chess, backgammon, and other games. With more than ten million books sold, we know what our customers want. Trust us.

3. THIS ONE IS A SURPRISE
Visit us now to get the goods!

So what are you waiting for?
CARDOZA PUBLISHING ONLINE